...more FAN-CARVING

by
Sally and David Nye

*Respectfully,
Sally Nye
David Nye*

**Published by Fan Carver's World
2160 66th St.
Fennville, MI 49408
Phone: 269.543.4755**

This book, **...more FAN-CARVING**, is published by Fan Carver's World. All rights reserved. No part of this work may be reproduced or used in any way, be it graphic, electronic or mechanical, including photocopying or information storage and retrieval systems without written permission from the copyright holder. The templates included herein are for the purchaser of this book to use for the purpose of learning how to do this type of woodcarving. The templates and/or other parts of this book are not to be duplicated for resale or distribution under any circumstances. Any such copying is a violation of copyright laws.

The tools suggested for use in this book could inflict injury or bodily harm if used improperly. The authors and publisher of this book are not responsible and disclaim any liability for any injury and/or losses that may incur from the woodcarving procedures stated herein. They encourage at all times the use of protective gloves, thumb guards and the knowledge, understanding and practical application of sound safety procedures.

```
Publisher's Cataloging-In-Publication Data
(Prepared by The Donohue Group, Inc.)


Nye, Sally.
   --more fan-carving / by Sally and David Nye.

      p. : ill. ; cm.

   Includes bibliographical references.
   ISBN: 978-0-9744464-1-7

1. Wood-carving.  2. Birds in art.  3. Fans.  I. Nye, David.  II. Title.  III.
Title: More fan-carving   IV. Title: Fan-carving

TT199.7 .N945 2007
736/.4                                                              2007904817
```

Publisher:	Fan Carver's World
Researchers & Authors:	Sally & David Nye
Carvers:	Sally & David Nye
Photographer:	David Nye
Illustrator:	Susan Harring
Graphic Designer:	Susan Harring

Copyrighted 2007 © Fan Carver's World

ISBN 978-0-9744464-1-7

Library of Congress Control Number: 2007904817

Fan Carver's World
2160 66th St.
Fennville, MI 49408
Tel: 269.543.4755
Email: sally@fancarversworld.com
www.FanCarversWorld.com

For books, tools, white cedar blanks or *questions* associated with fan-carving contact Fan Carver's World.

FAN-CARVING is a full-color 72-page book devoted to the Old World folk art of fan-carving.

It contains:
- European legends, customs and history.
- A comprehensive guide to wood selection and how to work with it.
- Step-by-step instructions and photos on how to make fans and fan birds.
- Full scale templates of a fan plus 5 different birds.

We are honored and proud to state that our books are produced in their entirety in the **U.S.A.**

Contents

Introduction		5
Chapter 1	More Fan Bird History	7
	Trench Art	17
Chapter 2	Santa and Old World Fan Carvers	19
Chapter 3	Wood Basics	33
	Adequate Moisture Content	36
Chapter 4	Wood Performance	39
	Wood Performance Experiments	40
Chapter 5	Fundamentals of Fan-Carving	47
	Fan Designs	71
Chapter 6	More Fan-Carving Patterns	72
	More Creations	135
Chapter 7	More Rived Items	136
Chapter 8	Oops ...but it's OK	138
Bibliography		142

...Patterns

Basic Fan pg. 49

Hummingbird
(with one fan) pg. 72

Hummingbird
(with three fans) pg. 72

Introduction

Typically, when one hears the word, "fan-carving," one thinks of fan birds. Fan bird history and the technique of making the fan bird was documented in our first book **FAN-CARVING**. *More* history, *more* experiments and *more* patterns are emphasized in this book **...more FAN-CARVING**. It also includes *more* information on the technique of fan-carving: the art of slicing long-fibered wood into blades and then turning and interlocking them to create a 3-dimensional design.

This book is an extension of our first book. There, we stated that the fan-carved bird originated in Russia and moved west to the Scandinavian and European countries. In **...more FAN-CARVING**, there is more in-depth history of the fan bird and more documentation of its symbolism. Insight on *how* this bird may have migrated from one country to another is most interesting.

A hundred years ago, the fan bird was relatively common. The skill of making the fan bird was passed down from one generation to the next. Today, however, fan carvers in Europe and Scandinavia are *few* in number. In fact, we didn't find any in Germany or Austria. The Old World fan carvers we interviewed for this book represent Finland, Sweden, Romania and Slovenia.

Every fan carver has to do the same basic cuts regardless of the style of his or her carving. These essential cuts are *riving wood*, the *hinge cut* and the *interlock cut*. The chapter on **Fundamentals of Fan-Carving** carefully explains *how* and *why* each cut is made. To better demonstrate this, a fan is made with step-by-step instructions.

Mistakes can and do occur with the novice carver. For this, four pages of **Oops...but it's OK** are devoted to *what* mistakes can happen and *why* they do. Here, instead of discarding their work, carvers will learn that fan-carving can be *very* forgiving.

To better guide fan carvers in their search for wood in their locale, we evaluated eighteen species of wood. Each one was rated for getting the blank from the round, workability, riving value, and turning value. A fan was made from each type of wood. Our recommendations are found in the chapter on **Wood Performance**.

Because adequate moisture content is *most* important for the turning of blades/feathers in fan-carving, an informative synopsis is in the chapter on **Wood Basics**.

Once the fan-carving process is understood and the technique mastered, the chapter on **Patterns** comes alive. There are 17 amazing creations! Each has full-scale illustrations with step-by-step instructions. These new designs include angels, butterflies, a peacock, a turkey, ladies, stars, honeybees, a flower and more.

In addition, there are two pages of **...more Rived Items**. They lack a hinge and an interlock, but such items can compliment the fan carver's gallery.

It is our hope that these new creations will inspire fan carvers to be even more creative and pass on their knowledge and skill to others. It is through them that this Old World folk art will live on.

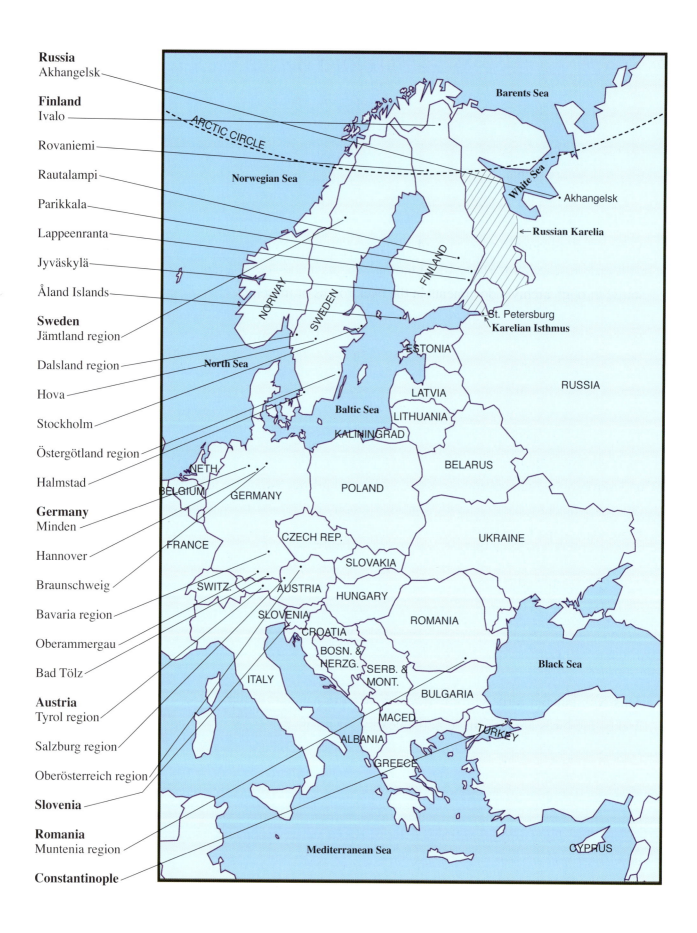

More Fan Bird History
Chapter One

For us, the search for fan bird history has been both challenging and exciting. In the beginning, little did we know that it would take us on a journey through Scandinavia and Europe and into a time capsule of four hundred years or longer.

Throughout this journey, we crossed mountain ranges, worked through language barriers, met with local research librarians, sifted through papers and books in antiquarian bookstores, and sorted through archival documents in the back rooms of museums.

We also interviewed museum curators, ethnographic experts, university professors and fan carvers. Whilst our adventure has been educational and fun, most importantly it has been very gratifying and productive.

This chapter on fan bird history is a continuation of the adventure which began in our first book, *FAN-CARVING*. There, we stated that the Old World folk art of fan-carving came from Russia and moved west to the Scandinavian countries of Finland, Sweden, and Norway. It also moved through the central and southern European countries of Poland, Slovakia, Austria, Germany, Romania and the Czech Republic.

Now, even with additional research, we still believe fan-carving originated in Russia. We can also speculate that the place of origin may be in or near Russian Karelia (including the Karelian Isthmus).* This area basically extends from Finland's eastern border to Russia's Arkhangelsk Oblast and from St. Petersburg in the south to the White Sea.

This Russian fan bird is from Arkhangelsk, Russia. Today, fan birds are also made in the nearby towns of Kargopol and Velsk.

*In brief: This area of Russian Karelia was part of the larger Karelian region. It is here where the Finns can trace their past to the 9th Century. Continuous wars and conflicts over this area have been common since the 16th century. It was under Swedish domination in the 17th Century, but in 1721, it was ceded to Russia by Sweden. Russian Karelia has been under the control and/or became part of Finland, Sweden, Germany and Russia at one time or another. This area is now part of Russia. The defeat of Finland by Russia in the Continuation War (1941-44) brought this Karelian region back under Russian control. Because of this, we say the place of origin of the fan bird is "Russia."

Upon the European continent, the fan bird dove is known by many names: Holy Spirit, Holy Ghost, bird of inspiration, dove-of-peace, ceiling bird, Christmas bird, chip dove, cuckoo, Easter bird, spirit bird, Christmas dove, dove of baptism, ceiling dove, whittled bird, wooden dove, ceiling cuckoo, cuckoo of Karelia, Karelian cuckoo, chip cuckoo, Christmas cockbird, Christmas pigeon, splint bird, etc.

Traditionally, the fan bird is hung in the home by a string so that it may move freely with air currents. It seems to come alive and symbolizes the Holy Spirit, protection, health, and happiness for the family. Customs about the bird may vary in different parts of Europe and Scandinavia. Some are more of a religious symbol than others, but all are about happiness, protection and good health.

The bird, but the *dove* in particular, has been a symbol for most religions and other belief systems since the beginning of time. As Christendom came into being, they too used the dove as a symbol in their religion.

As time went on, Christian leaders became concerned about the use of the *dove* as a Christian symbol because other religions or pagan beliefs had used it as well. Because of this, the Christian leaders gathered to discuss this crucial matter. The meeting took place in Constantinople in the year 536 A.D. It was here that the Council of Constantinople decreed that henceforth the *dove* can truly be used as a Christian symbol.

Thus, in 536, the dove officially became the symbol of the Holy Spirit. Since that time, as we all know, the dove has appeared as a Christian symbol in religious artwork.

The wooden dove shown on the Swedish postage stamp represents the Holy Spirit, a Christian symbol in Sweden. In the 17th century the dove fan bird was found in most churches. It hung directly over the minister's head. It was hung with a string from the pulpit, hence the name "pulpit bird."

The original bird that was the inspiration for this stamp was found in Hogsters Parish Farm, Dalsland, Sweden. The Nordiska Museet (museum) in Stockholm, Sweden, purchased it and then commissioned fan carver Einar Mellgren of Fagerlid, Sweden to make a replica. This replica was used for the motif for this stamp.

Today in the Swedish churches, the fan bird dove no longer hangs under the pulpit canopy. In its place, as a symbol of the Holy Spirit, is a solid wooden dove. This dove is in the pulpit of the St. Nikolas Church in Halmstad, Sweden.

Wooden dove under the pulpit canopy

Being an early church, St. Nikolas may have had a fan bird dove at one time. We do not know. Construction on the Church began in the 14th century and was completed in the 15th century. In 1619, Halmstad experienced a devastating fire that took most of the city. The St. Nikolas church was damaged but not destroyed.

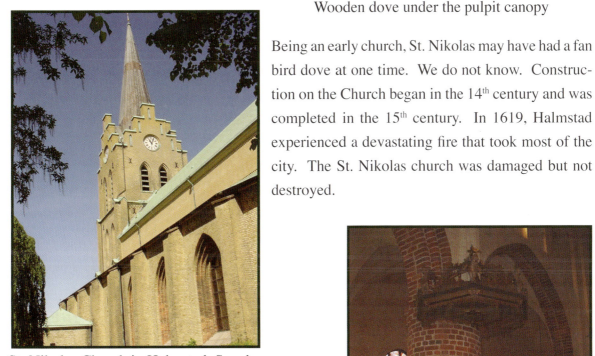

St. Nikolas Church in Halmstad, Sweden

After the fire, the mayor presented this pulpit (as a gift) to the church. It is still in use today. Pulpits of this type were introduced into the churches of Scandinavia and Europe in the early 1600's.

Note: Author David Nye's great grandfather's family attended the St. Nikolas church in the later part of the 1800's and early 1900's.

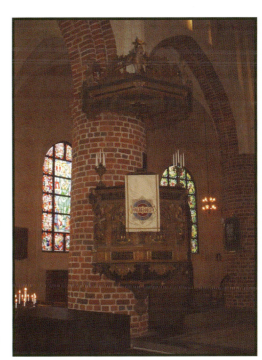

Pulpit within St. Nikolas Church

Traditionally, the wooden fan dove was also hung in the Swedish homes as a symbol of the Holy Spirit. In those early times, it was primarily hung at Christmas time, hence the name *Christmas dove*. It was also called the *ceiling bird* because it was hung from the ceiling. The bird was commonly placed over the dining-room table near lighted candles or over a stove. The warm air streams from the heat source caused the bird to slowly turn. Thus, giving the impression of being alive.

Reading the Gospel at Christmas
by Anders Montan, 1878
Nordiska Museum, Stockholm, Sweden
(Exhibit Nm 118 008)

Was the dove first in the church and then adopted in the home or did it migrate from the home to the church? We don't know.

In addition to the pulpit bird, there was another fan bird of religious significance …the Pelican. It symbolized *Christ*.

In 1913, a Swedish pelican bird was purchased by the Nordiska Museet (museum) in Stockholm, Sweden. This bird was from the parish of Hycklinge in the province of Östergötland, Sweden. The wings of this pelican bird were in a vertical position, which made it look more like a peacock. The "pelican" stamp (below) was based on a replica made by Einar Mellgren.

The wooden bird on the stamp symbolizes the pelican bird.* It was typical to find the pelican as part of the christening font in the churches. A pelican feeding its young with blood from its own breast symbolizes the all-sacrificing love and the redemption. The *pelican* symbolizes Christ, whereas, the *pulpit dove* symbolizes the Holy Spirit.

*Pelicans as christian symbols were written about as early as the 2nd century. Reference to them can be found in the *Physiologus*, an early christian work of Alexandria, Egypt. Since that time, there are variations of the legend but they are similar: *The baby pelicans die and after three days of mourning, the parent pelican pecks its own breast until there is a stream of blood. The babies take the blood and are revived.* In some legends the parent will die to save its young. However, even though there are variations, *all* of the legends symbolize the redemption and the all-sacrificing love.

Christening font

A more common image of the pelican bird at the Christening font is shown on this postcard of the Åre gamla Church (Sweden).

Åre gamla Church, Jämtland, Sweden

This pelican, feeding its young with blood from its own breast, is in the Heimatmuseum in Oberammergau, Germany.

Thord Mellgren of Hova, Sweden, made this Pelican fan bird. The pelican fan bird of this type is more often found in the northern part of the European continent. Thord has been making fan birds for fifty years. He and his brother Sig learned this craft from their father Einar Mellgren (born 1908).

Einar Mellgren was well known for his Swedish handicrafts which included fan-carving. He and his three brothers learned fan-carving from their father who learned it from a wandering Russian. From the time Einar was a young man to the late 1970's, he carved fan birds and other similar handicrafts. It was Einar who made the replicas for the two Swedish fan bird stamps of 1981.

Sweden is not the only country to commemorate the fan bird with postage stamps. Finland issued a fan bird dove stamp in 1985 and a stamp in 2000 featuring the Kökars Kyrka (Kökars Church in Åland). The cachet on the Åland first day cover shows the pelican fan bird feeding its young. We think the pelican bird was found in the Kökars Church that was built in 1784 on Hamnö Island, Åland (Finland).

Note: Our research seems to indicate that north of the Baltic Sea, the fan bird represented Christmas and to the south it represented Easter.

These fan birds are from the Peuran Museo in Rautalampi, Finland. They were made from several pieces of wood, as were other early European birds.

Eero Nokelainen was born in 1901 in Parikkala, Finland. Parikkala is near the Russian border in the South Karelian province. During the communist revolution (1917), many Russian people fled across the border into Finland. It was one of these Russian refugees that taught Eero how to make the fan bird in 1919-1920.

At that time, it was typical to make the bird by using four pieces of wood. However, due to the depression of the 1920's and the lack of employment, Eero soon developed his own technique of making a bird from one piece of wood. Today, the beautifully styled fan bird that is called the *Karelian cuckoo* is patterned after Eero's design.

Eero was considered the handyman of Parikkala. The townsfolk only had to state what they wanted and Eero could make it. In this manner, he provided for his family of 13 children. Many of these handicrafts were sold door-to-door …fan bird included.

 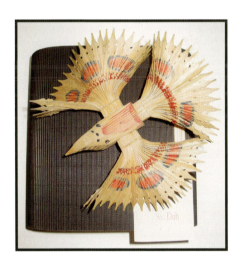

Two fan birds in the Slovenian Ethnographic Museum in Ljubljana, Slovenia symbolizing the "Zvaty Duch" (Holy Spirit.) Traditionally, these fan bird doves were hung by a string from the ceiling, over the table in the main room of the house. The other end of the string was attached to the door of the main entrance. When the door opened, the dove moving up and down would greet the guest.

Because the fan bird was always suspended, a person would have to *look up* to see it. Therefore, the bottom side of the bird would be most visible. It is not common to see a painted fan bird. However, if one is, it would be painted on the bottom side.

Top view of fan bird

Bottom side of same bird

This is the case of this fan bird from the Tirolver Volkunst Museum in Innsbruck, Austria. It was copied from one found in a private chapel near Schwaz, Austria.

Just prior to the 1900's, throughout western Austria (Tyrol, Salzburg, Oberösterreich), it was common to see the Holy Ghost/Spirit in the form of a wooden fan bird dove. Our research shows that farmers had the fan bird in their private chapels or altars. The dove was also found in the homes suspended above the dining table …as part of the "God-center."

Note: The God-center seems to be traditional of many European countries and/or regions. It is a place on the wall, in the living/dining area of the home that holds the crucifix and holy pictures. One turns to the God-center before and after mealtime.

Both of these fan birds are in the Tirvoler Volkunst Museum in Innsbruck, Austria. The one on the left is from the eastern part of North Tyrol, Austria, (exhibit #9021). The bird on the right (exhibit #2602) has no information.

In Austria, the Holy Spirit dove is also expressed in a "painted" form in the center of the ceiling. Painted sunbeams extend from the bird all the way to the walls. Whether the dove was painted on the ceiling or a wooden bird hanging with a string, it was the *protector* from the center *sky* of the room.

It is interesting to note that another custom in Germany (near Munich) and in Slovenia (country south of Austria) was the same: the bird is suspended in the center of the room and is also attached to the entrance door of the home by a string. When someone enters, it swings back and forth and therefore, serves as a greeting. But, the German bird was made of woven textile and not of wood. Depending on the time period and the region, the dove was sometimes made from woven fabric, blown eggs with paper wings, folded paper or carved from wood. However, the meaning was consistent …the *Holy-Ghost-dove*.

The wooden *fan style* dove was preferred in northern Germany. Archival records show that the Mindener Museum in Minden has at least two fan bird doves. These birds are of the typical European style made from three or four pieces of wood.

Typically, in evangelical regions such as Bavaria and northern Germany, the dove was made in the same wooden fan style. However, as in many regions throughout Europe, the religious influence of the bird faded through time and it became more of a decoration as we see in today's world.

This fan bird, in the Städtisches Museum in Braunschweig, Germany (exhibit #CD32) was found in a stable. Mr. Andree, curator of the museum (1904), brought it from Bad Tölz (southern Germany). Its purpose was to protect the stable animals from "evil-spirits."

An example of a fan bird with no meaningful symbolism is this one found in the early 1900's near Hannover, Germany. To Heinrich Korbes, the farmer who made it, it was just a toy.

In summary, fan birds representing both the dove and the pelican have been found in many parts of the European continent and Scandinavia. They represented religious symbols in the churches and homes, while others were merely a decorative item.

The "fan bird" is truly an Old World folk art that encompassed vast regions and all kinds of people. By 1900, the fan bird was so common that N.E. Hammarstadt (the famous Swedish ethnographer) called it a *cultural phenomenon*. These birds were found in the homes of the peasant as well as the elite. They were even displayed in the public rooms of government buildings. This phenomenon extended from the villages of the fertile farmlands to the tiny huts high in the mountain ranges.

But, how this bird may have migrated from one region to another is interesting. Our research through all of these countries revealed one common link …the soldier! Since the 16th century, continuous wars and conflicts over this area (Europe and Scandinavia) have been common. The movement of soldiers through these regions brought many cultures together. This *encounter* with different ideas, handicrafts, and skills forever changed *all* involved.

This photograph shows six soldiers on the Karelian front during the Continuation War between Finland and Russia (1941-44). As you can see, they are carving wooden buckets in their off-time. Items made by soldiers are often referred to as *trench art*. This photo is featured in the book *Muisto Syväriltä*, Sota-ajan Puhdetyöt, Finnish Trench Art by Liisa ja Tim Steffa, 1981.

...Trench Art

This fan-in-bottle is an example of souvenirs made by soldiers during World War I. The blades of the fan are of European style and the bottle is from the early 20th century or earlier. This is representative of World War I *trench art*.

Trench art refers to items made by soldiers at idle moments during wartime. A multitude of things were made which helped to relieve the stress of war, as well as boredom and homesickness. They used whatever materials they had at hand, such as spent shell casings and other battlefield debris. These trench art *creations* were often sold or used for barter.

From wood, soldiers made cups, spoons, ladles, canes, baskets, toys and even *fan birds*. Metal jewelry, knives, scabbards, etc, were also made when scrape metal was available.

The term *trench art* originated in France during the early years of World War I when trench warfare was prevalent. Today, soldier souvenirs from most wars are called *trench art* and are very collectible.

The soldier's skill to make these items was primarily based on old handicraft traditions that had been passed down through generations. Therefore, trench art is essentially a form of folk art.

It is also interesting to report that our research reveals that most of the senior carvers we met, learned the skill from the soldiers of World War II. A former World War II German soldier told us that he remembers seeing Russian prisoners-of-war making fan birds in Germany. Fan birds as *trench art*, are pictured in German and Finnish books that we found in antiquarian bookstores.

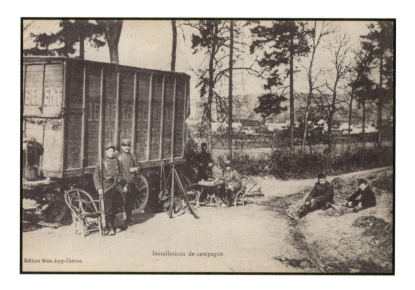

Because wars have had a profound impact upon this area (Europe, Scandinavia, and Russia), fan-carving history was also impacted. We know that World War II, in particular, helped spread fan-carving throughout Scandinavia and eastern Europe.

It can be documented that soldiers from both sides made fan birds. They taught one another and even the prisoners-of-war. Since troops moved from one area to another, one can easily understand how fan-carving spread across vast regions.

However, because of the devastation of World War II, fan-carving has almost become a lost folk art in all of Europe and Scandinavia. During the war, making a bird gave the soldier inspiration and/or cigarette money. After the war, it may have helped the carver/refugee feed his family.

As time went on and better jobs opened up, the carvers gradually set the fan bird aside. Sadly, in a few European countries today, there are no fan birds except in their museums.

Santa and Old World Fan Carvers
Chapter Two

Santa says, "Fan birds probably traveled by sea."

While traveling to Lapland to visit fan carver, Lintu-Antti, we stopped in Rovaniemi to visit Santa's village at the Arctic Circle in Finland. Because it was summer solstice and Santa was not busy, we had a wonderful conversation with him. When he realized we were in Finland researching the fan bird and its history, he offered his thoughts. We were pleased to find that Santa Claus is quite a historian.

Santa explained it is his belief that the fan bird is of Russian origin and is hundreds of years old. It probably traveled by water from Arkhangelsk, Russia (a major port on the White Sea). Historically, most trade routes followed the waterways. It was typical for the trade ships to follow the northern coastline of Scandinavia in order to reach the southern Scandinavian ports and those in the Baltic Sea (as did the Vikings). Thus, it is quite possible the early fan bird migration was by water.

...Finland

Lintu-Antti Turkia
Ivalo, Kuukkelilampi
Finland

Lintu-Antti lives in Lapland on lake Kuukkelilampi. He is a legendary fan carver as well as owner/manager of a recreational winter resort. Most of the buildings are "Kotas" (traditional round Lapland design). What a picturesque setting ...in the land of reindeer and Santa Claus!

From his Lapland resort, Lintu-Antti has sold thousands of fan birds. People travel great distances to see him make fan birds and taste his exquisite food. He is a person par excellence "legendary fan carver, chef, entertainer."

Lintu-Antti was born in 1941 and raised in Lappeenranta, Finland. It is the capital of South Karelia which is near the Russian border in southeast Finland. It was here where Lintu-Antti (age 9) learned how to make fan birds. His teacher was Aatos Partanen.

He remembers the lumberjacks of the 1950's and 60's carving fan birds in the evening hours. They were the Karelian cuckoo birds and each man had his own style. These "camp" birds were known to bring *Good Luck*.

Joel Nokelainen
Karjalohja
Finland

Joel Nokelainen lives in Karjalohja, Finland. He has been carving Karelian cuckoo fan birds most of his life. Pine and spruce are his preferred wood. He and his brothers learned the skill from their father, Eero Nokelainen. As a child, the youngest of 13, Joel helped his father sell birds door-to-door.

While watching Joel create a fan bird, it is apparent he inherited his father's skill. His hands move with adeptness and ease. It is a miracle to see the graceful Karelian cuckoo emerge from one piece of wood …in 6 minutes!

The fan bird has had a huge impact on Joel's life. In 1966, as a young man, he bicycled to Norway. Along the way he made and sold fan birds. Joel has also traveled with the fan bird to Germany, Switzerland, Denmark, Canada, Holland and Australia. It is his passion to preserve this unique skill.

Arto Ronkainen
Keminmaa
Finland

Arto Ronkainen's interest in fan birds began a few years ago when he saw a man making them. To see a knife used to *split* wood fibers was of interest because making the Finnish Puukko (knives) is Arto's primary business. In fact, he has won awards for his excellence in workmanship (www.apr-tuote.com).

Arto soon learned how to make fan birds. With each bird he includes a condensed version of a Finnish story about a bird:

"From the branches of the tree, the birds fly away. The tree, rooted in the ground, is left wondering, *if only I could fly like that…like a bird…to raise so high*. Nearly a thousand years time went by until one day a Lapis man took a knife and carved a bird from that tree …the wish fulfilled!"

Viktor Hukka
Kerkonjoensuu
Finland

Viktor Hukka began fan-carving after he retired a few years ago. His teacher was Kauko Rossi of Suonenjoki. Mr. Rossi is noted for his woodworking and carving skills and for teaching others this knowledge.

Viktor learned well! He is very adept at fan-carving. He also makes fir trees, sheep, roosters, hedgehogs, winter sun symbols, baskctry, and almost anything made from rived wood.

Note: See pages 136-37 ...More Rived Items.

Heikki Niskanen
Siilinjärvi
Finland

Heikki Niskanen saw his first fan bird when he was 9 years old. It was hanging in a small cabin and it captivated the young lad's soul. He devoted that evening (and many more) trying to understand and master the technique of fan-carving. That was 30 years ago.

Heikki makes fan birds as well as the Saint Tuomas Cross. This has been his full-time career for many years. When he demonstrates fan-carving, he attracts a crowd. When the bird is finished, he sets his knife aside and plays a tune on his accordion. Heikki is a crowd pleaser!

Professor Janne Vilkuna
Department of Museology
University of Jyväskylä
Jyväskylä, Finland

Sally Nye
Author: Fan-Carving
Fennville, Michigan, U.S.A.

Professor Janne Vilkuna teaches Museology at the University of Jyväskylä in Jyväskylä, Finland. He has been invaluable to our fan bird research. Professor Vilkuna explained that the place of origin of the fan bird is difficult to determine. This is due to the numerous wars and conflicts on the European continent during the 16th and 17th centuries (mainly between Sweden and Russia).

In the 17th century Sweden controlled Finland, Estonia and parts of today's Latvia, Denmark, Germany and Russia. There was constant struggle over territory and boundary lines changed continuously. Soldiers throughout Europe were always on the move.

Professor Vilkuna theorizes that it is quite possible the bird migrated with the soldiers. As the soldiers returned home, they brought with them the fan bird that they saw in the conquered lands. But *where* that was, one can only speculate.

Photos of fan birds: The flying fan bird is the same as the one on the table. Once it is hung, it really does look like its flying. This bird, from Professor Vilkuna's collection, is from an area northeast of St. Petersburg in Russia Karelia.

We asked Professor Vilkuna, "If the fan bird symbolism could be stated in one word, what would that be?" He said, "Peace or happiness! Everyone wants Peace and happiness."

...Sweden

Thord Mellgren
Hova
Sweden

Thord Mellgren lives in Hova, Sweden. He comes from a family of fan carvers. Thord is the third generation and learned the technique from his father, Einar. This is the same Einar who produced the fan bird replicas for the Swedish postage stamps in 1981.

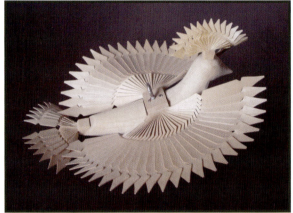

Thord has been making fan birds for 50 years. He supplies the Swedish market places with his delicate fan carved items: birds of many styles, stars, and angels. Even though he comes from a line of fan carvers, including uncles and cousins, we believe that Thord is the only fan carver in Sweden today. It is our hope that this old Swedish folk art continues and does not fade away.

More creations by Thord Mellgren (fan bird and angel).

...Romania

Dan Gherasimescu
Jud. Arges
Muntenia
Romania

Dan Gherasimescu is the President of the Romanian Woodcarving Association and is a fan carver. Today, there are only three fan carvers in Romania. Dan states that there are various traditions associated with the Romanian fan bird. As is common, it is known by many names. For example:

The fan bird symbolizes the Holy Spirit. It is called "the Soul Bird." It is customary to hang the *soul bird* over the child's bed and/or place it on the Christmas tree.

Another name is "the Sun Bird." Legend has it that the *sun bird* picks up the sun in the morning, carries it across the sky, and deposits it at sunset.

Another legend associates the fan bird with Dragobete Day, 24 February, the day of lovers (like Valentine's Day). It is also "the day when the birds are getting engaged."

...Slovenia

Bogomir Samec
Trbovlje
Slovenia

Bogomir Samec made his first Holy Spirit bird at the young age of 13 years. But there was quite a long time he did not carve the wooden bird. During the communist reign, it was not allowed because of the name, *Holy Spirit*. Bogomir carved other things and even moved to Germany for a while to escape the communist rule.

It was quite important to have the Holy Spirit fan bird in one's home. Bogomir said that many years ago, beggars would look into the window to see if there was a fan bird. It meant the master was a kind person and would provide help.

Bogomir has been carving for 50 years. He has taught other people how to do the Holy Spirit bird in order to preserve the Slovenian tradition.

Andrej Ozebek
Mošnje, Radovljica
Slovenia

Andrej Ozebek has been carving the Holy Spirit fan bird for 20 years. It all began when a museum asked if he could duplicate one that was found in their archives. The wooden bird was in pieces and was estimated to be 150 years old. Andrej carefully examined the wooden bird and determined how it was made.

Bird with 9-inch wing span

Through his ingenuity, he was able to reproduce the bird. Since that time, Andrej has been making the Holy Spirit fan bird. There was a time during the communist reign when it was inappropriate. During that time, he carved other things.

It is a Slovenian custom to give the Holy Spirit bird as a wedding gift. For this occasion, Andrej carves a bird holding a wedding ring in its beak.

Robert Perko
Monika Klememčič
Breznica
Slovenia

Robert, Monika and son Jiri, live in a small mountaintop village in Slovenia. From their cozy home they carve the traditional Holy Spirit fan birds. Each bird is carved with heartfelt humility and passion. And that is reflected in their lifestyle.

They explain that many years ago, beggars would carve these birds for homeowners as an offer of thankfulness for food, drink and a night's shelter.

It is said the Holy Spirit bird brings blessings and well-being to the home. The bird is suspended from a string that is attached to the door of the main entrance. As the door opens and closes, the bird ascends and descends. It is a greeting! In this manner, it welcomes the person who enters. It also serves as a doorbell to alert the homeowner that someone has entered.

Primož Korosec
Bohinjska Bistrica, Radovljica
Slovenia

Primož Korosec creates each piece of jewelry with heartfelt humility and passion as do Monika and Robert. They are friends!

Primož knows the Holy Spirit bird as "Messenger-of-the-Light." He explains that Light carries brightness, which gives life. Brightness is a living being. It gathers all wisdom of the universe and stretches to every space. It searches out corners of darkness and replaces the shadows with Light.

A white cedar swamp in northern Michigan. The cedar tree on the right would be a good specimen for fan-carving because of its straight bark. The tree on the left has too much twist.

Wood Basics
Chapter Three

Chapters 3 and 4 of our first book, **FAN-CARVING**, included extensive information about wood selection, wood characteristics, cutting trees, rounds, and getting blanks out. This information is summarized below.

...selecting wood

When selecting wood for fan-carving there are two main prerequisites. The wood must be straight-grained and also be long-fibered. For example, the type of wood used for making baskets will work for fan-carving.

Straight-grain and long-fibers are essential to make the thin blades that are necessary for fan-carving. To make thin blades, the long-fibers must be split. This process is called *riving*. To rive wood is to split or cleave the fibers. In short, the knife follows the fiber and therefore separates it from the adjoining fiber.

In summary, the knife separates the fibers while following the path of least resistance along the length of the grain without cutting through the fiber. It is impossible to make straight blades with fibers that are not straight.

Also, long-fibers insure the structural integrity at the base of each individually rived blade. Thus guaranteeing the fibers to hold as the blades are turned and interlocked. This is what makes fan-carving unique from other forms of woodcarving.

...what kind of wood?

Our wood of choice is white cedar that is found in the northern regions of the U.S.A. In central Europe, fir, spruce, and willow are preferred. Pine and aspen are favored in Scandinavia.

We want people to be able to use wood from their region. If it is straight-grained and long-fibered, we encourage them to give it a try. It is for this reason that we evaluated 18 different species of wood in our experiment on wood performance (pgs. 40-46). Each species was rated for its workability, splitting value, getting blanks out, and turning value. Hopefully, this wood performance experiment will offer suggestions and recommendations for fan carvers.

...from a tree to a round

Select a tree that has straight-grain and long-fibers. It should be at least 8 to 10-inches in diameter and have straight bark. If the bark is straight, it is a good clue that the interior grain and fibers are straight as well.

White Cedar tree

The log is cut into 5-inch rounds. This is because our templates are 5-inches long. That dimension is the length of the blank. A blank is the piece of wood used for fan-carving. In most instances, our blanks will be 2-inches wide by 1/2-inch deep and 5-inches long (2″ x 1/2″ x 5″).

...sapwood blank

The preferred wood for the blank is the sapwood of the round. This is the layer of wood just inside the bark and cambium layer. It is usually lighter in color than the interior heartwood. Sapwood is the active wood that contains the sap or lifeblood of the tree. It is softer to carve than heartwood.

Also, the annual growth rings of the sapwood are usually narrower than the heartwood. Blanks with narrow growth rings offer optimum performance for fan-carving. If given a choice of wood selection, choose sapwood with the tightest (narrowest) annual growth rings.

Note: A blank containing half sapwood and half heartwood offers a wonderful two-color effect to your fan-carving.

...getting the blank from the round

Place the tip of a large kitchen knife 1/2 to 3/4-inch in from the outer bark. With a mallet, give the knife a solid whack to cause a score about 1-inch in length. It does not need to be long.

Now, move the knife 2-inches from the first score and make a second score.

To get the blank out of the round, use a long handled screwdriver and mallet. Tap the screwdriver along a line about 3/4-inch in from the bark, between the two score lines. Do this until the blank begins to separate from the wood. A final whack with a screwdriver and mallet near the center of the crevice will free the blank from the round.

To retrieve more blanks from the round, continue the previous process. The best blanks are from the outer sapwood ring. Blanks from the second ring (heartwood) will work for fan-carving, but not as well.

Note: If you come to a knot, do not ignore it. Blanks with knots can make unusual creations. However, the fan/blade end must have straight fibers.

After removing the blanks from the round, use a hatchet to remove the bark from the blanks.

Smooth the blanks to your specifications with a roughing knife. Once the blanks are shaped, proper moisture content must be considered for them to be used for fan-carving.

...Adequate moisture content

The blank used for fan-carving must have adequate moisture content. This is paramount so the blades can turn at the hinge without breaking. It is one of the elements that makes fan-carving unique. To insure the blank has sufficient moisture, here are some options:

A. Take blanks from a live tree during the springtime when it is full of sap. Most likely it will have enough moisture.
B. Carve and rive the blank when it is dry. But before the blades are turned and interlocked, wet the hinge. To achieve this, spray water onto the hinge or soak the blank. In short, moisture is needed at the hinge for the blades to turn.
C. Boil the blank so there is adequate moisture throughout the blank for the entire fan-carving process.

Option C (boiling the blank) is our preference for the following reasons:
* The wood is softer to carve.
* The fibers split more easily when riving.
* It is easier to make thin blades.
* The wet hinge allows the blades to turn so they can be interlocked.

As we stated earlier, we prefer to use the sapwood of the tree. The advantage of the sapwood is that the cellular structure lends itself to moisture retention. Even if a tree has been down for several months, the sapwood will absorb moisture more readily than the heartwood.

Since hot water penetrates wood better than cold water, we boil the blanks to insure optimum moisture content. The blanks are submerged in a pot of water (with bricks or rocks placed on top). When the water reaches the boiling point, the heat is reduced and the blanks simmer for two hours. Essentially, we are permeating the blanks (wood fibers) with water.

Note: It is best to have ventilation when boiling white cedar. Some people have sensitivities to the smell.

Once the two-hour duration is over, the pot is removed from the heat source. The water is cooled and replaced with fresh water. The blanks will soak in fresh water for a day or two. This will allow for more water absorption.

The blanks are then cleaned of loose cambrian fibers and placed in double plastic bags. They are stored in the freezer for future use. It is best to use them within the year. To thaw for carving, place the blank in hot water for 5 to 10 minutes or set out overnight.

Every fan carver experiments with wood preparation in regard to proper moisture content. Some carvers boil the blanks until they sink to the bottom of the pot. For them, the wood has absorbed enough moisture for fan-carving.

Others leave the blanks in the water indefinitely. They select a blank from the bucket when they are ready to carve. We did this in the beginning but found that the wood turns a darker color and takes on a slime and foul odor. The wood fibers also become soft and mushy. It is for these reasons that we prefer the boil/freeze method.

It is not necessary to complete your fan-carving in one sitting. If you are interrupted, place the blank under the faucet for a quick rinse and put it in a plastic bag. Store it in the refrigerator until time to carve again. The water will be absorbed back into the blank. If you can't get back to your carving for a few weeks, it is best to place it in the freezer.

Note: After four or five months in the freezer, blanks tend to turn a darker color and dry out a little. Once they are thawed, place some water in the bag for a few hours to reconstitute the wood before carving.

Various tree species found on the authors' property.

Wood Performance
Chapter Four

Our wood of choice is white cedar. Being long-fibered and straight-grained, it is ideal for fan-carving. It grows in our area, but only as a shrub. To find white cedar with the required specifications for fan-carving, we must travel north 200 miles or further.

How wonderful it would be to have wood of choice at hand!

To help people find wood that may be readily available to them, we suggest:
- Try wood that is used for making baskets. It is noted for its long-fibers.
- Try wood from the genus Pinus (family Pinaceae): cedar, pine, fir, spruce.
- Try aspen. It is used in Finland.
- Try cypress. We used it in Florida.
- Try any wood that has long-fibers and is straight-grained.

To better guide fan-carvers in their search for wood, we did an *experiment of wood performance*. Eighteen species of wood were evaluated for fan-carving. Each one was rated for getting the blank from the round, workability, riving value, and turning value. A fan was made from each type of wood.

We purposely chose a wide variety of wood with anticipation of some failures. In fact, we were hoping for some. We wanted to show why some species would not work for fan-carving. However, it did not turn out that way. No failures resulted.

For that reason, we have to add the following disclaimer: *because Sally is experienced at riving wood, it appears she can rive almost anything*! However, just because wood can be rived, it doesn't mean we would recommend it for fan-carving.

Another disclaimer: It is important to realize that the same species of wood from two different regions can perform differently. In fact, we have found that wood from the same tree can perform differently. For example, white cedar is usually very soft to carve. However, it is not uncommon to find one side of the tree as hard to carve as maple or walnut.

Note: With that understood, don't take our experiment as fact. We encourage all carvers to experiment with wood in their area.

...Wood performance experiments

A. **Getting blanks from the round:** How well the pressure line follows the score line and annual growth ring. 1=good 5=poor
B. **Workability:** Ease with which the wood carves. 1=easy 5=difficult
C. **Riving value:** Ease with which the fibers split (straight and evenly.) 1=easy 5=difficult
D. **Turning value:** How well the fibers hold without the blades breaking off when they are turned at the hinge to be interlocked. 1=good 5=poor

...Wood that works well

American Quaking Aspen (Populus tremuloides)
Common names: trembling aspen, quaking aspen, golden aspen, mountain aspen, quiverleaf aspen, popple, trembling poplar and alamo blanco.

Getting blanks: 1
Workability: 2
Riving value: 1
Turning value: 1
Total: 5

Aspen performed very well in all categories. It was slightly harder to carve than our favorite, white cedar. **Recommended.**

Bald Cypress (Taxodium distichum)
Common names: bald cypress, southern cypress, swamp cypress, red cypress, yellow cypress, white cypress, tidewater red cypress and gulf cypress.

Getting blanks: 1
Workability: 2
Riving value: 1
Turning value: 1
Total: 5

Bald cypress was a bit hard to carve but its performance was very good in all other categories. **Recommended.**

Balsam Fir (Abies balsamea)

Getting blanks: 1
Workability: 1
Riving value: 1
Turning value: 1
Total: 4

Balsam fir was very nice to work with. While riving, some stringiness of the fibers occurred. They had to be cleaned off to avoid a messy appearance. For the most part, this is a nice problem because it translates to nice long-fibered wood. **Recommended.**

Black Willow (Salix nigra)

Common names: black willow, swamp willow, gooding willow and western black willow.

Getting blanks: 2
Workability: 1
Riving value: 1
Turning value: 1
Total: 5

Willow was very nice to carve and it was easy to rive. Due to the long fibers, it left quite a lot of "strings" to clean up but was not a problem. **Recommended.**

White Cedar/American Arbor-Vitae (Thuja occidentalis)

Getting blanks: 1
Workability: 1
Riving value: 1
Turning value: 1
Total: 4

White cedar is our favorite wood for fan-carving. It gives optimum performance in all categories. **Recommended.**

White Spruce (picea glauca)

Getting blanks: 1
Workability: 1
Riving value: 1
Turning value: 1
Total: 4

White spruce performed much like our favorite, white cedar. It was easy to carve and riving was fun to do. It preformed well throughout the entire process. **Recommended.**

...Wood that works, but not so well

Basswood (Tilia americana)

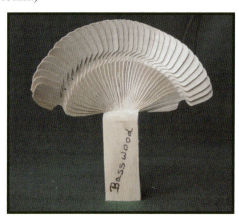

Getting blanks: 2
Workability: 2
Riving value: 2
Turning value: 1
Total: 7

Basswood rived O.K. but some fibers had ridges that were not consistent throughout the blank. However, that can be the nature of basswood. For that reason, we would **not recommend** it for fan-carving.

Buckeye (Aesculus pavia)
Common names: stinking buckeye and fetid buckeye.

Getting blanks:
  procured by
  another party.
  (est. 1-2)
Workability: 2
Riving value: 2
Turning value: 1
Total: 6 or 7

Buckeye was easy to carve for the most part. An oddity was the little pockets of very hard cells scattered throughout the blank. These spots caused difficulty during carving and riving. For that reason, some blades were lost. Therefore, we would **not recommend** it for fan-carving.

Pin Cherry (Prunus pensylvanica)

Getting blanks: 3
Workability: 3
Riving value: 2
Turning value: 1
Total: 9

Cherry was a bit hard to carve. It rived nicely and the blades held good while turning. It would **not** be our first or second choice for the "fun" and ease of carving.

...Wood that works hard (difficult)

Black Ash (Fraxinus nigra)
Common names: black ash, brown ash, basket ash and hoop ash.

Getting blanks: 3
Workability: 5
Riving value: 1
Turning value: 1
Total: 10

Black ash didn't follow the score line while getting the blank. Like white ash, it was very hard to carve but performed good for riving. Because it was so hard to carve, we would **not recommend** black ash.

White Ash (Fraxinus americana)
Common names: American ash, biltmore ash, small seed white ash and cane ash.

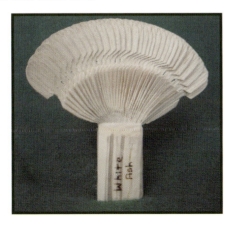

Getting blanks: 3
Workability: 5
Riving value: 1
Turning value: 1
Total: 10

White ash was difficult to get the blank out because the wood was so hard, but it followed the score line O.K. It was very hard to carve. However, it rived well and was actually fun to do. We see why this wood is used for the snowshoe industry. It splits well and is very tough/durable. Because it is so hard to carve, we would **not recommend** white ash for fan-carving.

White Birch (Betula Papyrifera)

Common names: paper birch, silver birch and canoe birch

Getting blanks: 4
Workability: 4
Riving value: 3
Turning value: 2
Total: 13

White birch was a problem. It did not follow the score when getting a blank from the round. It was hard to carve. It followed the fiber O.K. while riving but had some splintering. The blades were not as neat as yellow birch. **Not recommended.**

Yellow Birch (Betula lutea/alleghaniensis)

Common names: gray birch, silver birch, swamp birch, hard birch and curly birch.

Getting blanks: 3
Workability: 5
Riving value: 1
Turning value: 1
Total: 10

Yellow birch didn't follow the score line well. The bark was very difficult to peel—it had to be cut away. Muscle is needed to carve this wood! The redeeming factor is that it rived very nicely with no fiber stringiness. The interlocking was fun to do because of the sturdy blades. I would **not recommend** yellow birch because of its hardness. Other than that, its performance was fun.

...Hard wood that works hard

Black Walnut (Juglans nigra)

Getting blanks: 5
Workability: 5
Riving value: 4
Turning value: 2
Total: 16

Black walnut is hard to carve. It followed the fibers somewhat during riving. It was unruly! When turning the blades, some fell off. It is a difficult wood to work with. We would **not recommend** it for fan-carving.

Eastern Red Cedar (Juniperus virginiana)

Common names: eastern red cedar, Virginia juniper and eastern juniper.

Getting blanks: 5
Workability: 3
Riving value: 5
Turning value: 2
Total: 15

Red Cedar didn't follow the score lines when getting the blank out. Carving was O.K. During riving, red cedar revealed its temperamental personality. The fibers created their own ridges and truly controlled the knife (like trying to steer an auto equipped with power steering minus the steering fluid). Even though it is a visibly pleasing wood, we would **not recommend** red cedar.

Hemlock (Tsuga canadensis)

Common names: Canada hemlock and hemlock spruce.

Getting blanks: 5
Workability: 5
Riving value: 4
Turning value: 3
Total: 17

Hemlock is hard to carve. While riving, the fibers were inconsistent and felt warped and twisted. For that reason, the blades split thicker and some of them did not hold while turning. You can visually see the blades do not lay flat. We would **not recommend** hemlock.

Red Maple (Acer rubrum)

Getting blanks: 5
Workability: 5
Riving value: 3
Turning value: 3
Total: 16

Red maple didn't follow the score line when getting the blanks from the round. The wood was very hard to carve. While riving, the fibers felt "twisty." Red maple was temperamental to work with. **Not recommended.**

Sugar Maple (Acer saccharum)
Common name: Hard maple

Getting blanks: 5
Workability: 5
Riving value: 3
Turning value: 3
Total: 16

Sugar Maple did not follow the score line when getting the blanks. The wood was exceptionally hard to carve. It took muscle! Also, it was temperamental to rive. The knife had to be worked with the fiber all the way. Was this fun? NO! Will we try this again? We hope not! **Not recommended.**

Comment:
Even though we did not recommend many of the woods used in our experiment for fan-carving, it did reveal an amazing fact: fans can be made (however difficult) from many species of wood! This unexpected awareness afforded us new insight and more possibilities for fan-carving.

For example, a couple marries and plants a tree in honor of their wedding day. 50 years later the tree must be taken down. They want a *memento* made from the wood of that tree to commemorate their marriage. Is it possible to make a "fan or fan bird" from that piece of wood? We would say "yes." It may be difficult to make, but what a *memory* it would signify!

The top of each blade of this *momento* is heart-shaped. The heart/love theme is carried through into the handle.

Fundamentals of Fan-Carving
Chapter Five
...Recommended tools

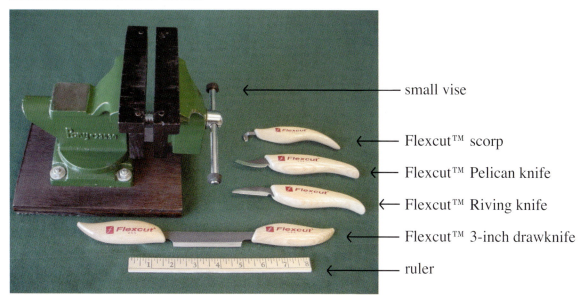

- small vise
- Flexcut™ scorp
- Flexcut™ Pelican knife
- Flexcut™ Riving knife
- Flexcut™ 3-inch drawknife
- ruler

small vise – device with two jaws that close together to hold a blank when it is rived/sliced into blades/feathers.

Flexcut™ scorp – small v-shaped gouge used for blade/feather decoration. Available for left-hand or right-hand.

Flexcut™ Pelican knife – knife with concave cutting edge used for carving.

Flexcut™ Riving knife – single-bevel knife used for riving/slicing small blanks when held in hand. Available for left-hand or right-hand.

Flexcut™ 3-inch drawknife – single-bevel drawknife with thin cutting edge used for riving/slicing blanks when held in a vise.

ruler – straight edge used for measuring or drawing lines.

Fan-carver's third-hand – device used to grasp small items, allowing both hands to be free for interlocking blades/feathers. Also see pg. 132.

For your protection, we recommend a kevlar glove on the hand holding the blank and a thumb guard on the other.

Fan-carver's *third-hand*

...Fundamentals

Chapters one and two show fan birds from many countries. The styles are as diverse as their cultures. Even within each culture, the fan carvers have their own style. Nevertheless, each fan carver has to do the same basic cuts:

1. Split the fibers to make a blade: rive the wood
2. Carve a narrow place for that blade to turn: the hinge
3. Carve a place for each blade to connect to the next one: the interlock

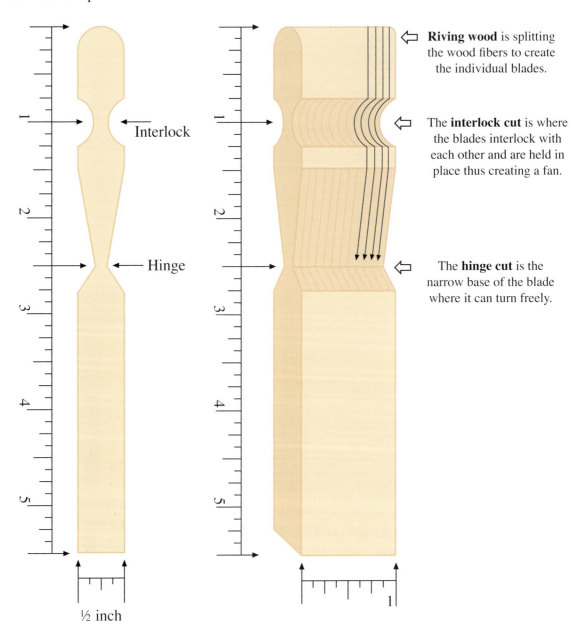

Riving wood is splitting the wood fibers to create the individual blades.

The **interlock cut** is where the blades interlock with each other and are held in place thus creating a fan.

The **hinge cut** is the narrow base of the blade where it can turn freely.

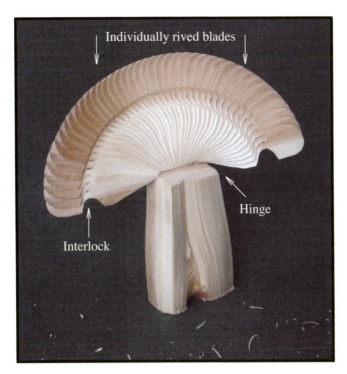

This white cedar fan exhibits the three basic cuts necessary for fan-carving:

- individually rived blades
- interlock cut
- hinge cut

Each of these cuts has a function. To become proficient at fan-carving, each cut must be properly executed. Therefore, it is important to understand:
  a. *How* these cuts are made.
  b. *Why* these cuts are made.

Each cut will be carefully explained and demonstrated by making a fan. With step-by-step instructions, the fan-carving process will be more easily understood.

For this project, a white cedar blank was used. It is two-colored: half sapwood (white) and half heartwood (honey-colored). It measures 1-inch across at the top and gradually widens to the bottom due to the knothole. It is also 1/2-inch deep and 5 1/2-inches long (1" x 1/2" x 5 1/2"). Sufficient moisture has been added.

Note: To understand proper moisture content, see pages 36-37.

Step 1 ...examining the blank

Front side

Back side

Examine the blank to determine the best layout for the fan. Choose the end with the straightest fibers for the fan blades.

Straight fibers are needed when splitting (riving) the wood fibers into individual fan blades. The knife will split the fibers (not cut through them). It will follow the fibers down to the hinge cut.

The other end of the blank will be used for the fan base or handle. This end may have a slight curve, wavy grain, discoloration or something unusual. However, these unusual creations of nature can often enhance the design.

In addition to being two-colored, this blank exhibits several unusual and natural characteristics:

- a knothole at the base.
- a shiny cambium layer on the front side.
- curved cedar fibers around the knothole.
- a wavy indentation projecting upward from the knot.

Ordinarily, this blank would be thrown away.

Step 2 ...squaring the blank

With a Flexcut™ Pelican knife or favorite whittling knife, trim the four sides of the blank so they are straight and uniform. However, try to preserve any natural characteristics. If possible, incorporate them into the design. In our case, because of its uniqueness, we will preserve the bottom portion of the blank.

With this blank, only the top portion will be squared off. That area will be for the fan blades.

Step 3 ...rounding the top

Round off the straight end of the blank. The rough end grain must be trimmed so that the top is round and smooth. This rounded end will be the tip of the blades. A rounded end is preferred over a pointed end.

Examine the top to insure it is round and smooth. A rounded end gives more surface area for gauging the thickness of the blade when slicing/riving.

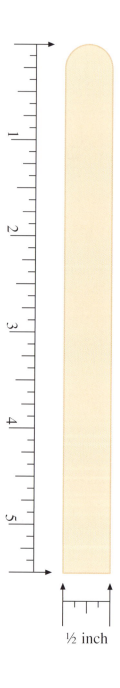

½ inch

Step 4 ...measuring for the interlock cut

Measure 1-inch from the rounded top and make a mark on one long side of the blank.

Do the same on the opposite side.

Draw a line to connect these two marks.

Repeat this on the other side of the blank so that the 1-inch line is on both sides of the blank.

This line will be for the interlock cut. Remember, the interlock cut is where the blades "interlock."

Step 5 ...carving the interlock

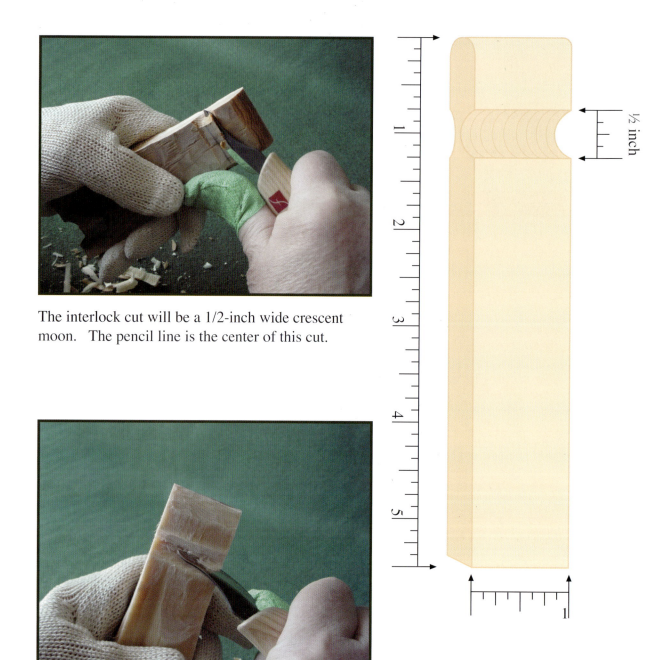

The interlock cut will be a 1/2-inch wide crescent moon. The pencil line is the center of this cut.

Remove 1/4-inch from each side of the line to make a C-shape (crescent moon).

Remove 1/3 of the wood from each side of the blank so that 1/3 is left in the center. This interlock cut is done on both sides of the blank. It is important that they are aligned when looking at the narrow side of the blank. The reason for this is that when the individual blades are turned and interlocked, they need to interlock securely and, as a result, will create a uniform pattern.

Also, it is best to work on both sides simultaneously and check often to insure your cuts are centered and aligned. Because if you work on only one side, it is easy to focus on that alone and get too far into the center. This would cause the center to be "off-center" and too narrow. It will also make the interlock weak and wobbly when slicing the blades.

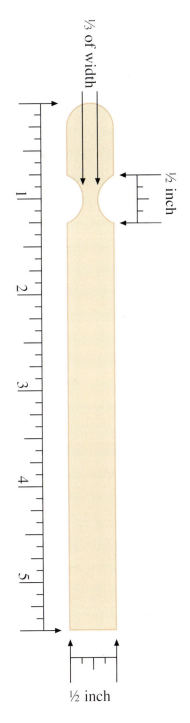

Step 6 ...measuring for the hinge cut

The next basic cut is the hinge. This is the base where the blades will turn so that they can interlock with the next one.

Measure 2 1/2-inches from the rounded top of the blank and make a mark.

Draw a line across the blank. Now, do the same measurements on the backside of the blank. This hinge line is where the blades will turn.

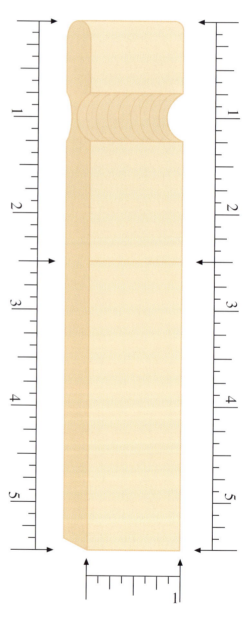

Step 7 ...maintaining a buffer zone

Measure about 1/4-inch beneath the interlock cut. This area acts as a buffer zone between the hinge cut and the interlock cut. It is best to leave this area intact.

Why is this important? The wood in this buffer is needed to separate the two cuts: the hinge and the interlock. It also gives structure and strength to the blades when they are interlocked.

It is best to draw a line showing this buffer so you do not cut into it.

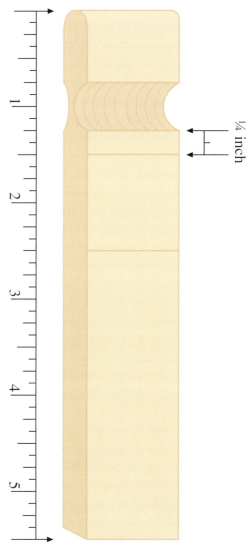

Step 8 ...carving the hinge

This cut is a long slanted cut. The taper begins just below the interlock buffer zone and extends to the hinge line. The other side of the hinge line has a very short taper.

In short, this is a V cut with a long side and a short side. Where they meet, it is important that this line (across the blank) remains straight and crisp.

Note: The Flexcut™ Pelican knife or a knife with a concave cutting edge really works best for this type of cut.

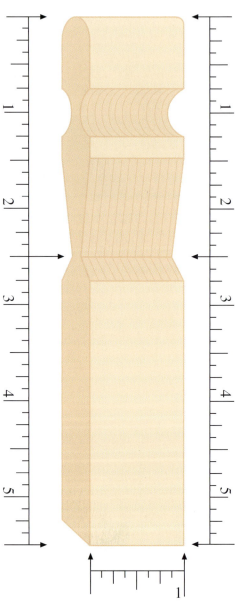

Start with a small V cut along the hinge line (the line being the point of the V). Cut towards the line.

It is important to work on both sides of the blank simultaneously. By doing so, it helps to insure that both sides are properly aligned and that the hinge is centered.

Continue to taper each side of the blank by always cutting towards the hinge line. Notice that the taper begins at the buffer line and stops at the hinge.

The hinge cut will serve as a stop-cut during the riving process. Because of this, it is important that a good straight line is maintained.

Notice the short taper cut. The slight taper is needed on the lower hinge cut so the blades will have freedom to curl away while riving.

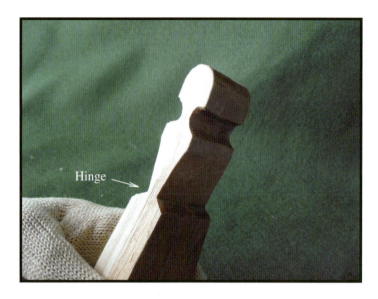

At this point the hinge should be about 1/8-inch in the center.

Note: This hinge cut will be made narrower after the blades are sliced. But for now, the 1/8-inch thickness is needed. This will give structural integrity to this area of the blank when rived.

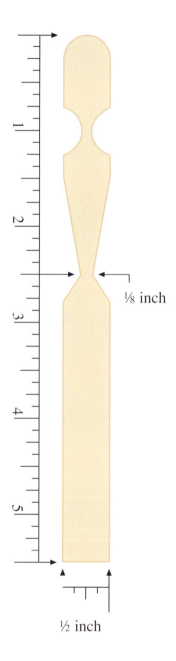

Step 9 ...riving the blades

The next step is splitting the fibers. This is called riving (with a long i).

But, before the blank is placed in the vise, check to see if there is a protruding feature such as this one. If so, trim it so that it is more uniform. An uneven blank can split when pressure is applied while tightening the vise. After all, this is long-fibered wet wood.

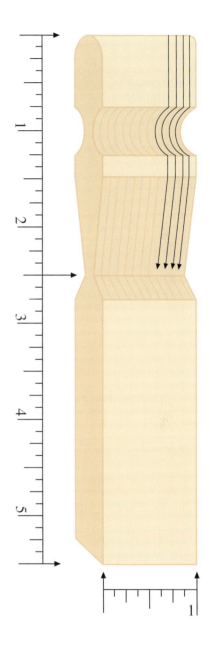

It is now time to rive the fibers (blades). The blank is clamped in the vise with the rounded side up. Rive from the front of the blank to the back (the front being the furthest away).

The Flexcut™ 3-inch drawknife is recommended for riving. It was designed for fan-carving. It has a flat back with a single-beveled edge. The flat back of the knife stabilizes the riving action, thus allowing the evenness of the blades down to the hinge. The single-bevel acts like a carpenter's plane when slicing thin blades.

The knife is used with the flat-back facing the carver. The single-bevel is on the opposite side of the knife. From this position the cutting edge cannot be seen.

Tip the knife backward to visually gauge the desired thickness of the fan blade. With the knife's edge still on the rounded top, seat it into the wood. Now, stand it straight up and…*slowly push down*. Gently push down to the hinge cut. Remember, the hinge cut is to serve as the stop cut.

While riving the first few slices, let the knife *find* the fiber line. It is O.K. if some of these fan blades fall away. In fact, it is uncommon to find the fiber line with the first few slices. Once found, uniform blades can be achieved.

Due to the narrowness of the interlock, the knife will go faster through this area because it is the point of least resistance. It is typical to become startled and lean forward causing the knife to tip. This can create a small gap between the back of the knife and the blank. A slight gap near the interlock will cause the knife to go *off-fiber*.

Note: Do not allow a gap to come between the back of the drawknife and the blank. If the fan blades are thin at the top and thick at the bottom, this is the reason. The cut is on an angle. It is paramount that this is corrected.

Rive the fibers straight down to the stop cut at the hinge. Trust the knife to follow the wood fibers. Ease of riving is the norm. Become familiar with *feeling* this splitting/riving action. If the carver leans over to watch it happen, it is almost certain the rive will go off-fiber.

The fan blade should easily peel away from the blank like shaving or peeling a piece of wood.

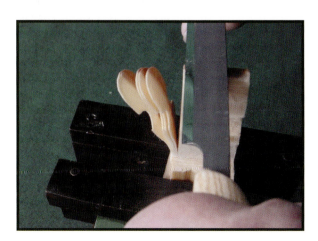

In short, keep the back of the drawknife tight to the blank and let the cutting edge move slowly down to the hinge while splitting the fibers.

Hint: Always strive for thin fan blades even if a few are lost. The loss will hardly be noticed when the blades are interlocked. Of course, if several are lost in a row, there will be a gap.

Step 10 ...narrowing the interlock

Once the riving is complete, look *through* the blades (front to back) at the interlock cut. Check to see if the crescent shape is uniform through all of the blades. If not, correct any lopsided or misaligned cuts.

The sides of the C-cut should have a very slight slope. This will allow the individual blades to turn and interlock with no interference with the adjoining blade. Also, by doing this, a nice and neat fan pattern will be created after all of the blades are interlocked.

Now, while holding the blades tightly together, trim the interlock more. A narrow interlock is preferred with thinner blades because it is necessary that they fit tightly together. With more blades per inch, they need to be interlocked in the least amount of space.

Check *often* by peaking through the blades to see that the interlock is centered and that the C-cut has a nice "cup" shape. This will allow the blades to fit tightly together when they are interlocked.

How narrow should the interlock be? It depends on how many blades there are. The more blades, the more narrow the interlock. A place must be created for them to find a home.

Note: The narrowness of the interlock becomes apparent with practice and by making thinner blades.

Step 11 ...narrowing the hinge

It is time to narrow the hinge. Remember, it was left wider before the blades were sliced. This was necessary to give structural integrity to the blank when riving. Now that the blades are sliced, the hinge needs to be more narrow so the blades will turn with ease and create a better design or pattern once they are interlocked. How narrow should the hinge be? ...about the thickness of a toothpick!

First, check the width of the hinge. Look through the blades down to the hinge to see how much narrower it should be. Also, see if the hinge is centered. If not, correct this while narrowing the hinge.

To do this, trim the long tapered side. It extends from the buffer to the hinge. Remember, work on both sides of the blank simultaneously.

Trim back to the hinge from the short side. Maintain a nice crisp line at the hinge.

Again, the hinge should be about the thickness of a toothpick.

Note: We know that at first it is frightening to make the hinge so narrow. But, through practice, confidence will prevail and the fear will fall away. By working with long-fibered wood and understanding its characteristics, you will soon learn that *long-fibered wood* is very forgiving for fan-carving.

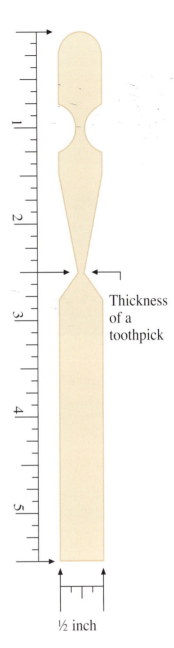

Thickness of a toothpick

½ inch

Step 12 ...shaping the handle

This is a good time to shape the handle of the fan. It is easier to do this before the blades are interlocked (fanned out). Because of the uniqueness of our blank, we have chosen to keep it natural. Therefore, no shaping will be done.

Step 13 ...flexing the blades

The blades should be flexed before they are turned and interlocked. This back and forth movement will loosen the fibers at the hinge. This will allow the blades to easily turn in a uniform manner. It will also help to insure that there is a nice crisp line at the hinge once the fan is interlocked.

When flexing the blades, snapping and popping sounds may be heard. This is O.K. It may seem that the blades will fall off. This will not happen unless the fibers have been cut through.

Step 14 ...interlocking the blades

The blades are ready to be turned and interlocked.

Grasp the first blade on an end. Turn and pull it away from the others.

Note: Whenever possible, it is best to handle the blades beneath the interlock ...that is the strongest part of the blade.

Do the same with the next blade and interlock the first and second blades together.

Continue interlocking the blades. Make sure they turn at the hinge.

As more blades are interlocked, notice an attractive fan pattern developing because of the narrowness of the interlock and the hinge.

Step 15 ...A Fan!

Front

Back

Once completed, position the fan to your liking. Set it aside to dry for a couple of days and then spray with a wood sealer. Enjoy your fan!

...Fan Designs

Two scorp cuts across the fan blades can create an intricate pattern. Once fanned out, the decorative detail is revealed. It is truly amazing what a *small nick* can do for fan designs.

On this fan, scorp cuts were made above and below the interlock, creating a unique design.

Here, the top of each blade is heart-shaped. The *love* theme is also incorporated into the handle.

Fan handle carved with a special person's initials.

The top of each blade is evergreen-shaped. The carved handle becomes the tree's trunk.

...More Fan-Carving Patterns
Chapter Six

Hummingbird with one fan

These hummingbirds are two different styles because of the way they were interlocked. The top bird has one continuous fan and the bottom bird has two wings and a tail. Actually, they are the *same* bird. After the photo was taken of the top bird, and while it was still wet, the feathers were unlocked. Then they were re-interlocked to form the bird below with three fans.

Hummingbird with three fans

Hummingbird

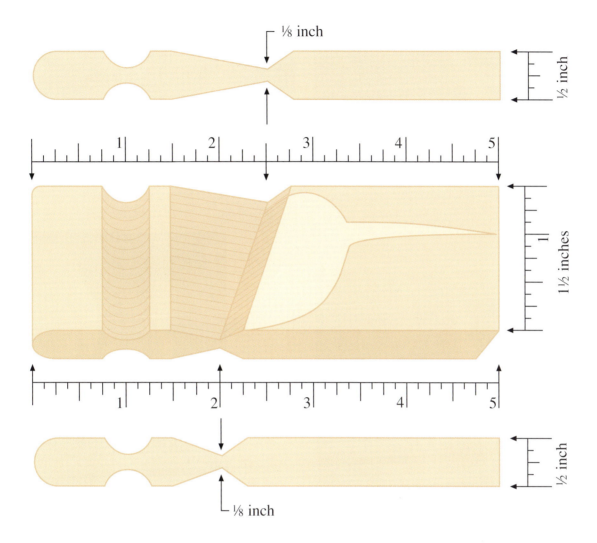

This blank is 1½″ x ½″ x 5″. Round off the end. It is the tip of the feathers.

Measure 1″ from the rounded end. Draw the interlock line.

Make the usual interlock cut (pg. 54).

Draw the hinge line: 2½″ at top and 2″ at bottom.

Make the buffer zone (pg. 57) and make the usual hinge cut (pg. 58).

Rive the feathers (pg. 61).

Narrow the interlock and hinge (pgs. 64-66).

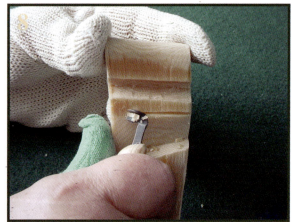
Make decorative cut with v-shaped scorp just under the buffer zone.

Trim the short side of the hinge cut. This allows a place for the feathers to be moved alongside of the bird's head.

Draw the bird's body onto the blank. Start carving the hummingbird's body. Cut off the end tail feather and round off the bird's bottom. Leave enough lower body to serve as a counter balance for the wings. This helps the bird to fly level.

Trim off the feathers behind the head. This allows the bird to have a nicely shaped head.

Continue carving the hummingbird, giving it a nice long beak.

Flex the feathers before interlocking (pg. 68). Start interlocking the feathers on the tail end (bottom). The last feather will serve as the center/anchor feather.

Interlock the second feather to one side of the anchor feather.

Interlock the third feather to the other side of the anchor feather.

Continue interlocking every other feather to its appropriate side until all are used. If one is left over, cut it off.

Using a needle-nose pliers and 20-gauge wire (or similar), make a small eyelet. Thread a string through the eyelet and insert it into the bird. It is nice to conceal it at the back of the head where the wings begin. Position the wings so they are aligned with the body. After the bird has dried, it can be sprayed with a sealer.

...interlocking feathers for two wings and a tail

Count an uneven number (7 or 9) of bottom feathers for the tail. Place a marker (wood chip) here to separate wing from tail feathers.

Move the first feather to one side of the bird's head.

Move the second feather to the other side of the bird's head.

Interlock the third feather with the first feather.

Continue interlocking alternately to build the two wings. Leave an uneven number for the tail (9 in this case).

To interlock the tail, use the last (bottom) feather as the anchor feather.

Interlock the second feather to one side of the anchor feather.

Interlock the third feather to the other side of the anchor feather.

Continue interlocking every other feather to the appropriate side until all are used. Position the wings and tail to be aligned with the body.

Love Gift Angel with Dove-of-Peace

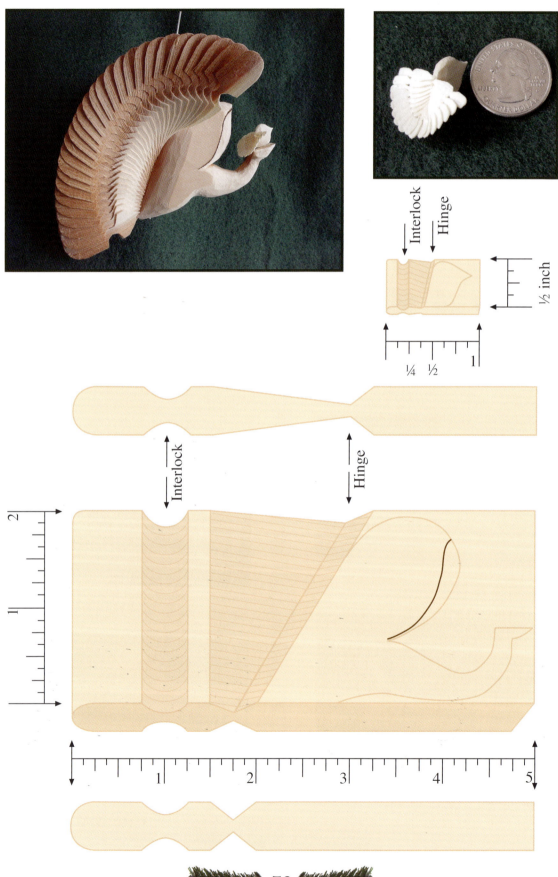

Draw the pattern onto the blank. The blank is 2″ x ½″ x 5″. It is two-colored: half sapwood and half heartwood.

Round off the tip of the wing feathers.

Make the usual interlock cut (pg. 54).

Mark the buffer zone (pg. 57) and make the usual hinge cut (pg. 58). It is 3″ on the head side: 1¾″ on the lower body side.

Rive the angel's wings (pg. 61).

Narrow the interlock and hinge (pgs. 64-66).

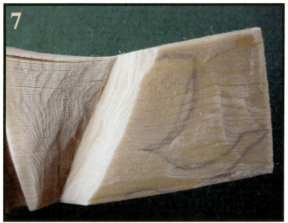
Trim the short side of the hinge cut.

Start carving the angel's body.

Continue carving the angel's body.

She will hold a *love gift* in her hands.

Flex the feathers. This loosens the fibers at the hinge. It allows the feathers to turn easily so they can be interlocked.

Move the first feather to one side of the angel's head.

Move the second feather to the other side of the angel's head. Interlock the third feather with the first feather.

Continue interlocking alternately to build the two wings.

Outline the angel's cloak by woodburning.

The Love Angel holding the *Dove-of-Peace* in her hands. Insert an eyelet as shown on pg. 76.

Love offerings, such as the *Dove-of-Peace*, can be placed in the hands of the Love Angel.

The illustration for these miniature birds is on page 78. Instructions to make them are the same as the hummingbirds (pg. 73). Follow those directions …but think *"small"* (½" x ¼" x 1").

Angel Gabriel with Horn

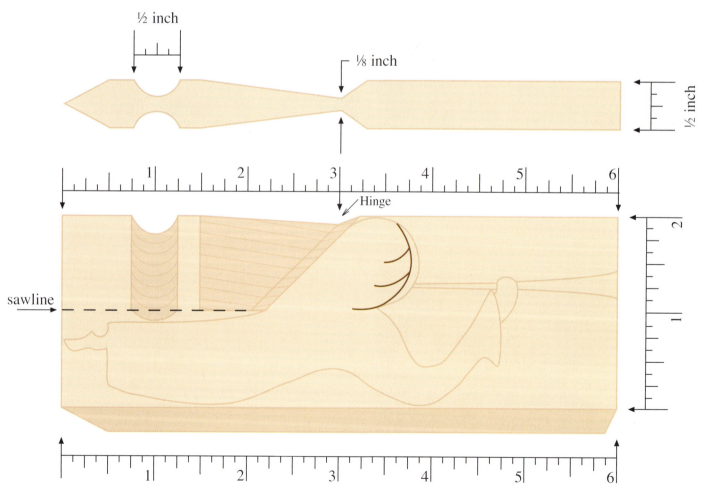

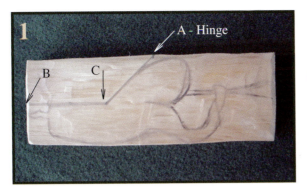

This blank is 2" x ½" x 6". It is two-colored: half sapwood and half heartwood.

Draw the illustrated pattern onto the blank while following these guidelines:

A - Along the 6-inch side that has been selected for the top (wings), make a mark at 3" (arrow A).

B - Measure 1" along the 2" side and make a mark (arrow B).

C - From there (B), draw a 2" line down the center of the blank (arrow C).

D - Now connect this line (C) with the 3" mark at the top of the blank (A). This is the hinge line.

E - Finish drawing the pattern by using the illustration or your own adaptation of the Angel Gabriel.

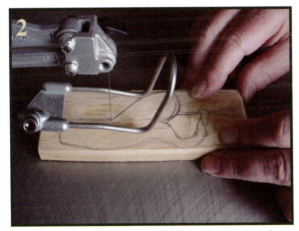

Saw along the 2" line (B to C), just to make a slice.

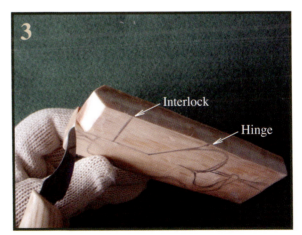

Shape the tip of the wings. A pointed tip is more appropriate for an angel. Draw the interlock line. It is 1" from the tip of the feathers.

Make the usual interlock cut (pg. 54).

Make the buffer zone (pg. 57) and carve the hinge cut (pg. 58).

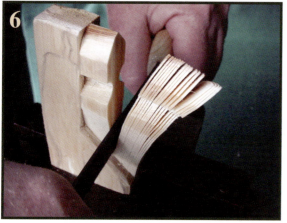

Rive the wing feathers (pg. 61). Trim the interlock and hinge some more. There is a lot of handling to do while carving the angel. This could weaken the hinge. So, do the final interlock and hinge trimming later.

Drill a hole in the crook of the arm. This offers a point to begin carving.

Cut off the rived feathers to form the back of the angel's head. This allows the wings to protrude more from the shoulder area and *not from* the back of the head.

Trim the short side of the hinge cut. This allows a place for the blades to pivot and interlock without butting against the wood that, in this case, will be Gabriel's back and shoulders. Also, begin carving the lower body.

Continue carving the angel's body. Keep things centered. Notice the alignment of the armpit, shoulder and head. Also, notice the relationship and alignment of the wings, mouth and horn.

Narrow the interlock and hinge for the final time (pgs. 64-66). Insure the shoulders (cloak) are smooth.

Flex the blades (pg. 68) and begin interlocking the angel's wings. Move the first feather to one side of the head.

Move the second feather to the opposite side.

Move feather number three and interlock it with number one.

Continue building the wings by interlocking every other feather to the appropriate side. If there is one left over, cut it off. Adjust the wings.

Make an eyelet using a needle-nose pliers and 20-gauge wire. Insert a string into the eyelet. Seat the eyelet into the damp wood in front of the wings (pg. 76). After Angel Gabriel dries, woodburn some wisps of hair (if desired). Spray with a sealer.

Peacock

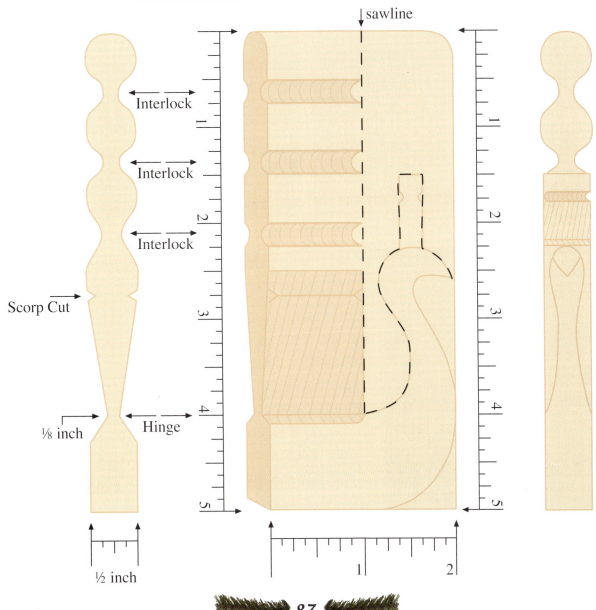

This blank is 2″ x ½″ x 5″. Draw the pattern onto the blank by following the illustration.

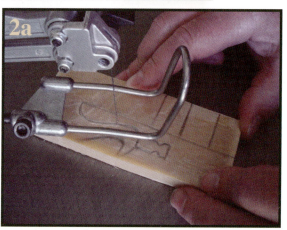

Saw along the dotted line with a scroll saw or similar device.

Round off the top of the tail feathers and roughly shape the interlocks. For a reference point, lightly mark ½-inch circles on the end. Peacocks are noted for their colorful circles (eyes) on their feathers. The three rounded interlocks on the tail represent these "eyes."

Attention: Be conscious that the wood is wet and long-fibered. The base of the blank (the peacock's body) is now only 1-inch tall and ½-inch wide. It can easily split! While carving, try not to apply undue pressure to the base. If it should split, don't throw it away. Try super glue.

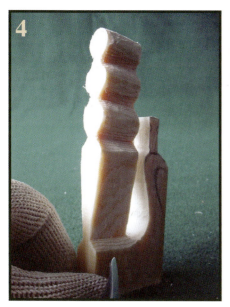

Shape the circles (eyes) of the feathers so they are rounded. The lower one is more difficult to execute due to the interference from the crest.

Mark the buffer zone (pg. 57) and make the usual hinge cut (pg. 58).

The crest is ½″ wide x ¼″ deep x ¾″ tall. Round off the top and draw the interlock lines.

Carve the crest's interlock and hinge.

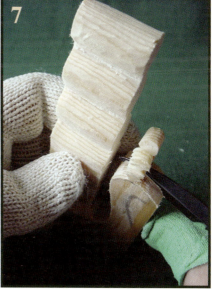

Rive the crest. The riving knife is used for small places such as this. It has a single-beveled edge that faces the carver.

89

Rive the tail feathers. Begin near the head and rive towards the tail end (pg. 61).

Carve the bird's body. Shape the chest so it is more rounded.

Narrow all of the interlocks and hinges on *both* the tail and the crest (pgs. 64-66). Trim the short side of the hinge cut so it blends into the body.

Make a scorp cut to *suggest* that the feather eyes continue down the tail.

Flex the feathers (pg. 68) and begin interlocking them with the tail end feather. This will be the center/anchor feather.

Interlock the second feather to one side of the anchor feather. This will be a **double** interlock.

a. The feather base will go *over* the anchor feather.

b. Place the bottom circle *under* the one on the anchor feather.

c. Place the middle circle *over* the anchor feather.

d. Place the top circle *under* the one on the anchor feather.

By weaving the feather back and forth, it will be interlocked in two places or more (depending on how you look at it).

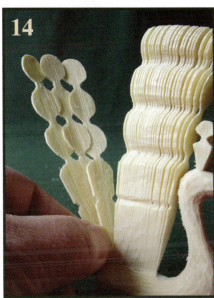

Interlock the third feather to the other side of the anchor feather in the same manner.

Continue to *double interlock* every other feather to its appropriate side until all are used. If one is left over, cut it off.

Interlock the crest as a fan (pg. 68).
Now the majestic peacock is displayed!

Strutting "Tom" Turkey

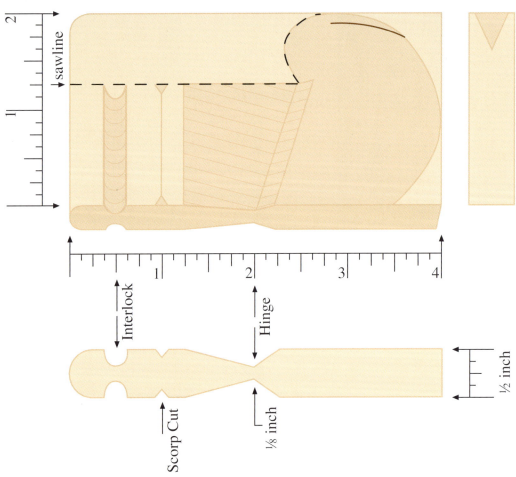

This blank is 2″ x ½″ x 4″.
Draw the pattern onto the blank.

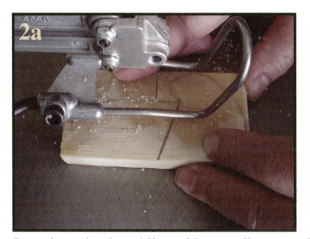 

Saw along the dotted line with a scroll saw or similar device.

Round off the top of the feathers.

Draw the interlock line ½″ down from the tip of the feathers.

Make the usual interlock cut (pg. 54). It will be ¼″ wide.

Make a scorp cut about ½″ below the interlock cut. This represents the *marking* that is characteristic of the turkey's tail feathers.

Draw a line ¼″ below the scorp cut for the buffer zone (pg. 57).

Carve the hinge (pg. 58).

Rive the tail feathers (pg 61).

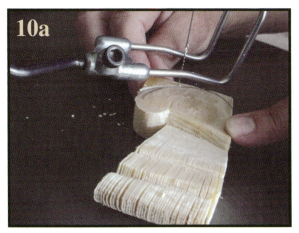 

Trim the body with a scroll saw or carving knife. Draw on the snood. This tom turkey is *strutting* so his head is tucked back.

Shape the body.

Trim the snood with a scorp. Then trim the lower edge with a knife to give the snood more definition.

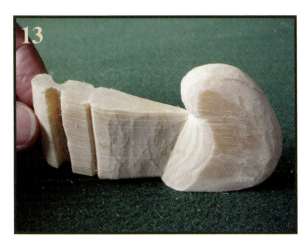

Narrow the interlock and the hinge (pgs. 64-66). Trim the lower edge of the hinge cut to blend into the turkey's body.

Begin interlocking the tail with the first feather behind the head. This will be the anchor/center feather.

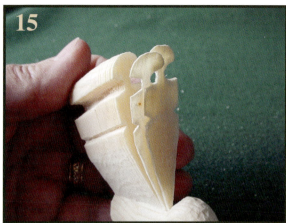
The second feather will interlock to one side of the anchor feather.

The third feather will interlock to the opposite side of the anchor feather.

Continue interlocking the feathers until all are used. If there is one left over, cut it off.

Woodburn along the snood.

Back view of strutting "Tom" turkey.

Indian with Headdress

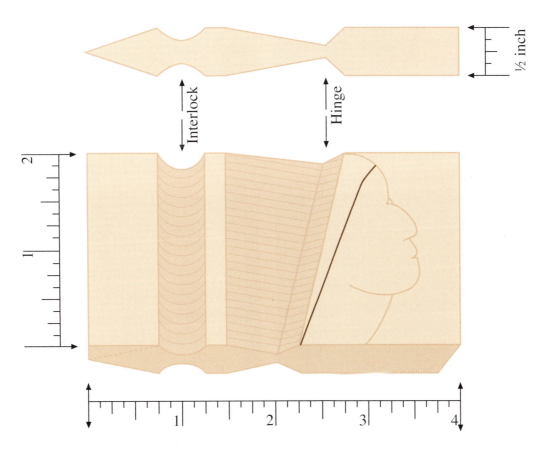

Interlock

Hinge

½ inch

97

Draw the pattern onto the blank. This blank is 2″ x ½″ x 4″.

Make a very pointed end. Also, carve the interlock 1-inch down from the top (pg. 54). The pointed end will taper all the way to the interlock.

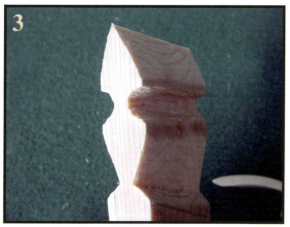
Mark the buffer zone (pg. 57) and make the usual hinge cut (pg. 58).

Rive the feathers (pg. 61).

Narrow the interlock and the hinge (pgs. 64-66).

Cut off the corners of the blank with a saw.

Rough out the profile of the face.

Carve the facial profile.

Woodburn the headband. Flex the feathers (pg. 68) and begin interlocking with the first feather at the top of the head. That will be the anchor/center feather. The second feather will interlock to one side of the anchor feather. The third feather will interlock to the opposite side of the anchor feather. Continue interlocking the feathers until the headdress is full.

Any remaining feathers can serve as a base to support the headdress.

Indian with headdress.

Pine Tree

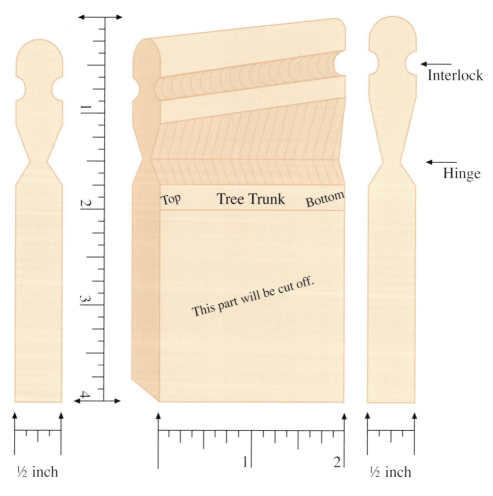

Interlock

Hinge

Top Tree Trunk Bottom

This part will be cut off.

½ inch

½ inch

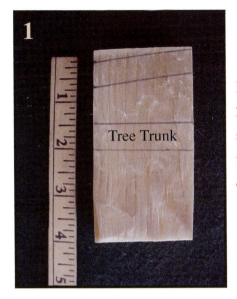

Draw the measurements onto the blank. This blank is 2" x ½" x 4". Notice the ¼" angle across the top. The shorter side is the tip of the shorter branches that are at the top of the pine tree. The longer side is the bottom end branches of the tree.

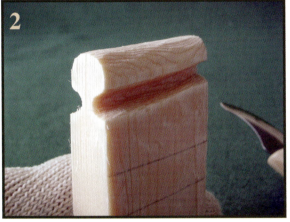

Round the angled top. That is the tip of the branches. Carve the interlock (pg. 54) ½" down from the top. It is ¼" wide.

Mark the buffer zone (pg. 57) and carve the hinge (pg. 58).

Rive the blades (pg. 61). Begin at the longer end. That is the base of the pine tree.

Narrow the interlock and the hinge (pgs. 64-66).

Trim the lower side of the hinge cut. Cut off a few blades on *both* ends of the tree. Flex the blades (pg 68).

Cut off the waste wood.

Rough out the tree trunk. Final shaping of the trunk can be done after it dries.

For ease of counting the blades, they are divided into groups of 10 blades each. The groupings are helpful when interlocking blades for the individual branches. The branches at the top of the tree will have fewer blades than those at the bottom.

Count an uneven number of blades for the bottom branch (in this case 21). It is the base and will support the tree so it can be freestanding. Begin interlocking with the top blade (#21) of that grouping. It will be the anchor/center blade.

 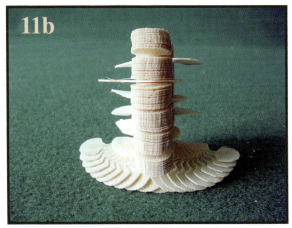

The second blade (toward the bottom) will interlock to one side of the anchor blade. The next blade will interlock to the opposite side of the anchor blade. Continue interlocking until all of those 21 *lower* blades are used. This is the lower branch (bough) of the pine tree.

Build the branches by interlocking the regular fan method (pg 68). Position each fan branch to the left and to the right so they resemble *pine boughs*. The fan *boughs* will be shorter in length and fewer in number toward the top of the tree. **Note:** The number of blades in each bough from bottom to top is 21-15-12-9-8-5-3.

Pine tree with seven boughs.

Lady with Parasol

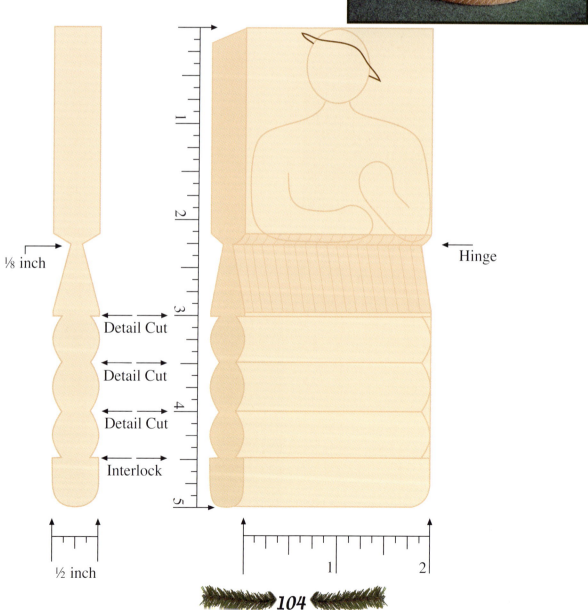

This blank is 2″ x ½″ x 5″. Draw the pattern onto the blank by following the illustration.

Round off the end. This is the bottom of the skirt.

Rough out the interlock and the *detail cuts* as shown in the photo. The *detail cuts* serve no functional purpose. They are for *fashionable* skirt design only.

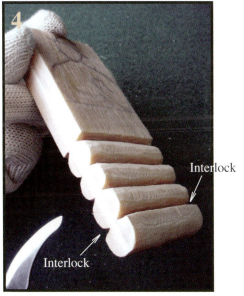

Continue to round off the *detail cuts* of the skirt. Notice that the interlock has one straight side (instead of the usual C-shape). The *detail cut* closest to the waistline also has a straight edge. This gives more definition to the finished skirt.

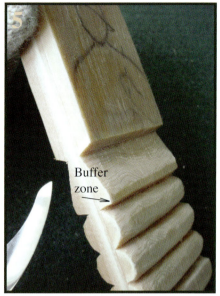

Notice the small buffer zone (pg. 57). Carve the hinge (pg. 58) and give the short side a slight angle.

Trim the edges around the shoulders and head. Leave enough wood so that the blank can be securely held while riving.

Rive the blades for the skirt (pg. 61).

The center 1-inch is the lady's waistline.

Trim off some outer blades but not to the 1-inch waistline (for now). Leave some extra blades in case they are damaged while carving the body. They will be cut off later.

Continue carving the lady. The angle of the shoulder and the hands must be in a line to hold the parasol. Carve deep enough so a hole for the parasol can be drilled through that line.

Drill a hole for the parasol.

Narrow the interlock that is at the bottom line of the skirt (pg. 64). Also, narrow the hinge at the waistline (pg. 66).

Cut off the outer blades so that the waistline is 1-inch.

Flex the blades back and forth so they will turn to interlock with ease.

Begin interlocking with an end blade.

Interlock the next one to the first one.

Continue interlocking the blades the same way until all are used.

Once completed, this style suggests "a lady *walking*."

If "a lady *standing*" is preferred, position the skirt so it is rounded in the front.

To maintain the shape of the skirt, place the lady in a vessel to dry. In this case, she is standing in a cup.

Or find a vessel with the proper diameter and secure her to it with a rubber band.

Lady with parasol.

Parasol

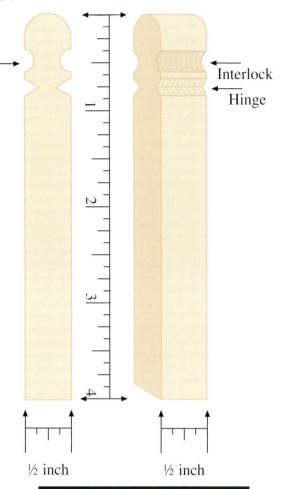

⅛ inch depth

Interlock
Hinge

½ inch   ½ inch

This blank is ½″ x ½″ x 4″. Round off the end. Mark the interlock at ½″ from that end. Also, mark the hinge at ¾″ from that end.

Carve the interlock (pg. 54). It is ¼″ C-shape and *only* ⅛″ deep. Also, carve the hinge (pg. 58).

Rive *thin* blades (pg. 89). The goal is to create the *most* blades in the *least* amount of space to form a circle. For small items like this, the riving knife works well.

Narrow the hinge, but **NOT** the interlock. The purpose of the wide area (centerwood) between the interlock cuts is so that a circle is formed once the blades are interlocked.

Narrow the parasol handle.

Flex the blades (pg. 68) and begin interlocking with the end blade.

Continue interlocking to form a circle.

The last blade can be bent over to complete that circle.

Top view of the parasol.

Handle view of parasol.

Trim the parasol handle so it fits through the drilled hole. Now you have "a lady with a parasol."

Stars

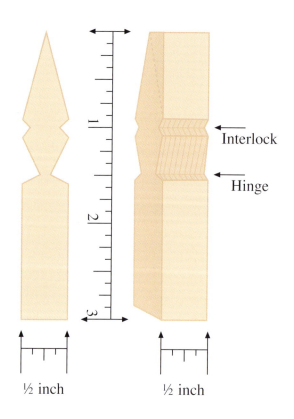

Interlock

Hinge

½ inch   ½ inch

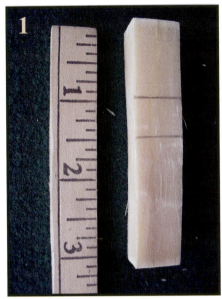

This blank is ½" x ½" x 3".
Draw the interlock at 1-inch.
Draw the hinge at 1½".

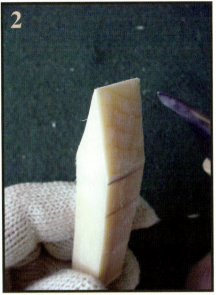

Make the end pointed. It will be tapered from the top end to the interlock.

Carve the interlock. It will be ⅛" V-shape (instead of C) and *only* ⅛" deep. The purpose of the wide area (centerwood) between the interlock cuts is so that a circle is formed once the blades are interlocked.

Carve the hinge (pg. 58).
There is very little buffer zone.

Rive the blades (pg. 89). Thinner is better, but when fanning circular patterns, it is *imperative*. The goal is to create the *most* blades in the *least* amount of space.

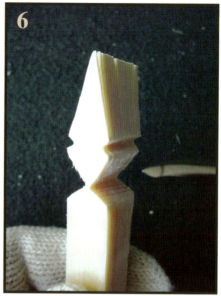

Narrow the hinge more. It must be *very* narrow.

Split the blank into two parts. Two stars can be made.

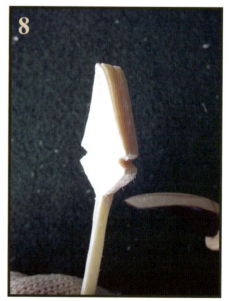

Trim the base.

Begin interlocking with the end blade.

Interlock the next blade to the first blade.

Continue interlocking until all blades are used.

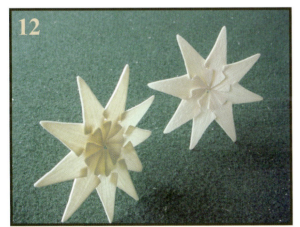

Both of these stars are made from the same blank that was split into two parts. One part had some inferior blades that were removed. This resulted in an 8-pointed star. The other part of the blank had more good blades. The interlock cuts were made deeper to accommodate them to form a circle. This resulted in a 10-pointed star.

Both stars ...different view.

Flower and Honeybee

Flower with twelve petals.

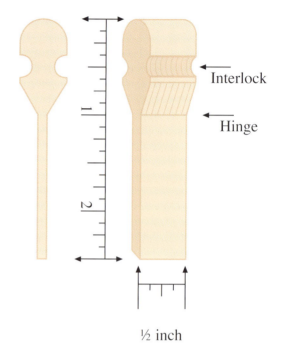

½ inch

At left, are two views of the same flower. The blank to create this *flower* is ½" x ½" x 2 ½". This pattern is a variety of the parasol (pg. 111) and the star (pg. 114). Use the same technique to make the flower.

Note: It is important that the interlock is only ⅛" deep. Remember, the purpose of the wide area (centerwood) between the interlock cuts is so that a circle is formed once the blades are interlocked. *Fan-carving is truly amazing!*

Honeybee and flower.

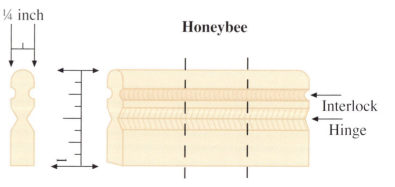

Honeybee

¼ inch

Save the small pieces of waste wood. Use them for making small fan-carved items such as honeybees. Split the ½" dimension into two ¼" pieces. Each blank is ¼" x 2" x 1" (at its shortest part). Three honeybees can be made from each blank.

It is easier to hold and carve a blank of this size and later divide it into three parts for the little honeybees. **Note:** It is better if the wood is *not* too wet. Being this narrow, it can easily split.

Round off the end. It is the tip of the wings. Draw the interlock line (¼" from the rounded end) and the hinge line (½" from the rounded end).

Carve the interlock (pg. 54). Mark a small buffer zone (pg. 57) and carve the hinge (pg. 58).

Rive the wings (pg 61). They are *only* ½" from top to bottom. Since many, many wings are to be rived, the blank can be placed in a vise and rived with a draw knife. Riving by hand with the riving knife is O.K. too (pg. 89). Use your preferred method.

Once rived, divide the blank into three parts. Three honeybees can be made.

Narrow the interlock and hinge (pgs. 64-66).

Begin shaping the bee's body. Cut off a few blades for the *head* and the *tail*.

Flex the blades (pg. 68) and interlock them to form two wings (pg. 71).

Release (cut) the honeybee from the blank. Finish shaping the bee's body.

Affix the honeybee to the flower with a drop of glue. **Note:** Since more bees can be made from the blank, a bee skep makes an attractive display (See pg. 135).

Sunbonnet Girl

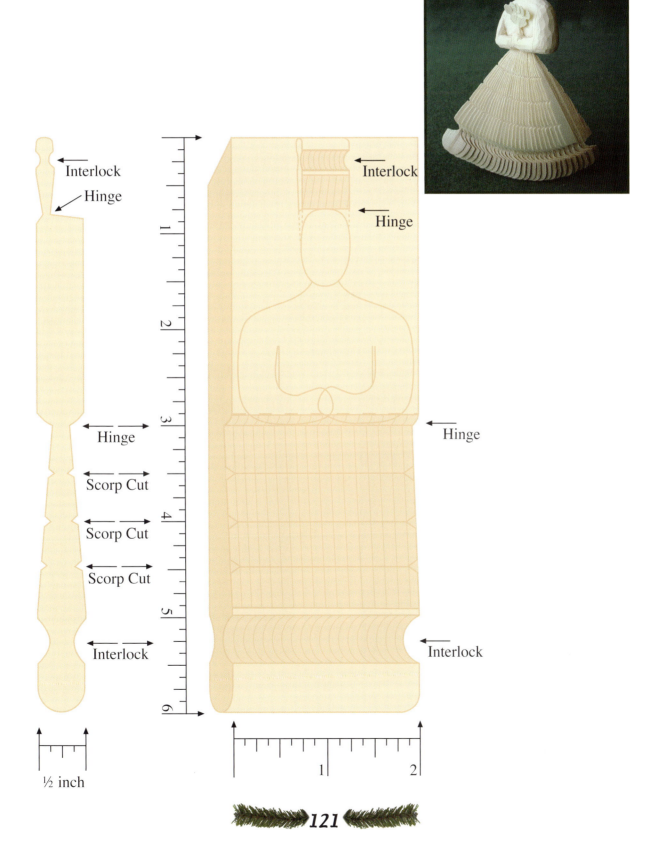

Interlock
Hinge
Hinge
Scorp Cut
Scorp Cut
Scorp Cut
Interlock

Interlock
Hinge
Hinge
Interlock

½ inch

Draw the pattern onto the blank by following the illustration. This blank is 2″ x ½″ x 6″. It is two-colored: half sapwood and half heartwood.

Round off the end. It is the hem of the skirt. Then carve the interlock (pg 54).

Carve the hinge (pg 58). The scorp lines are cut off and will be put back on later.

Rive the blades for the skirt (pg. 61).

Trim the waste wood around the head and sunbonnet.

Carve the sunbonnet. Round off the end and carve the interlock and the hinge (pgs. 54-58). Notice that it is placed at the back of the head. Because that part of the blank is *heartwood*, the sunbonnet will be honey-colored.

Rive the blades for the sunbonnet. The riving knife works well for small things such as this (pg. 89).

Start carving the head and upper body.

Continue carving the body. The head is slightly turned because she is walking in that direction. When carving the hands, leave room to make a small hole for a fan. (See pgs. 107-108).

Draw the scorp lines back onto the skirt and make those cuts.

Narrow the interlocks and hinges on the sunbonnet and the skirt (pgs. 64-66).

Flex the blades (pg. 68) and begin interlocking the skirt at one end. Use the basic fan method (pgs. 68-69).

To complete the skirt, continue interlocking the blades until all are used.

Interlock the bonnet using the same fan method.

Position the sunbonnet so that it bends forward from the hinge. A rubber band works well to secure it until it is dry.

The design on the skirt (scorp cuts) is appropriate for the *Sunbonnet Girl*. As an added feature, a small fan is placed in her hands.

Pisces

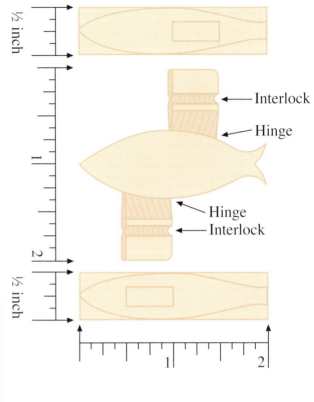

Draw the pattern onto the blank.
The blank is 2″ x ½″ x 2″.

Cut out the pattern with a saw.

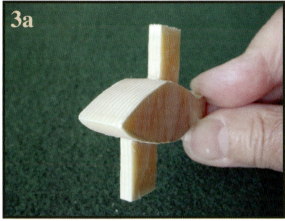 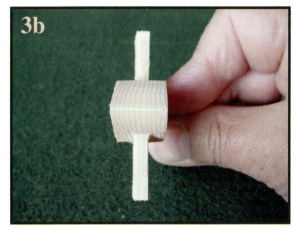

Narrow the top and bottom fins until they are ⅛″ thick. Both ⅛″ thick fins should be centered with the fish's body.

 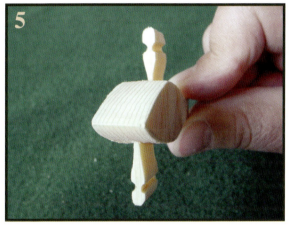

Round off the tips of both fins. Make the interlock cuts (pg 54). Both interlocks are ¼″ from the rounded end. The C-cuts are ⅛″ wide.

Make the hinge cut (pg. 58). Remember to check often so the fins are centered along the middle of the fish's body.

Rive the top fin (pg. 89). Start at the tail end. The rived blades will peel away in the direction of the tail. This helps the fin to lean toward the tail once interlocked.

Rive the bottom fin. Begin at the nose end. The interlocking will begin there.

Narrow the interlocks (pg. 64) and begin carving the fish's body. The hinge cut will be narrowed later …after the fish is carved.

Finish carving the fish and make the hinge cuts narrower (pg. 66). Because the wood is wet and carving is *with* the grain, the wood wants to *split* away in layers. The fish can be smoothed after it is dry. However, it is awkward to do once the three fins are interlocked.

Begin interlocking the top fin with the first blade nearest the tail. Interlock the second blade to the first and continue interlocking until the fin is complete. If there are too many blades, cut some off. **Note:** The Fan-carver's third-hand (as shown on pg. 47) securely held Pisces while his fins were being interlocked.

Begin interlocking the bottom fins by turning the first blade (closest to the nose) to one side. Turn the second blade to the opposite side. Interlock the third blade with the first blade. Continue interlocking alternately until the two fins are complete (pg. 77). If there are too many blades, cut some off.

Turn Pisces right side up. A fish with its *belly-up* is not a good sign.

Pisces complete with three fins.

The other side of Pisces.

Butterfly

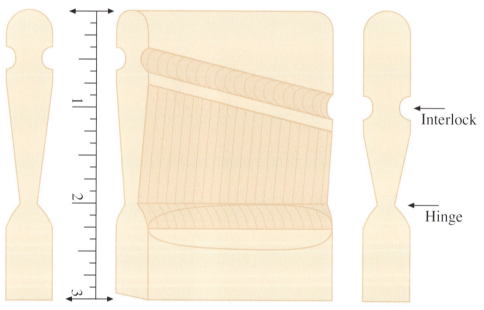

→ Interlock

→ Hinge

Draw the pattern onto the blank using the illustration. The blank is 2″ x ½″ x 3″.

Round off the end. It is the top of the wings.

Carve the interlock on an angle (½″ to 1″).

a. ½″ is the butterfly's tail side.

b. 1″ is the head side.

c. The interlock is ½″ wide.

Mark the buffer zone (pg. 57) and make the usual hinge cut (pg. 58). It is 2″ from the rounded end and is straight across the blank.

Rive the butterfly's wings (pg. 61).

Narrow the interlock and hinge (pgs. 64-66).

Make a scorp cut across the wings near the buffer zone. It is for detail only.

Trim the short side of the hinge. This is the butterfly's back and should blend into the body. Cut off a few blades on each end so the butterfly has a head and a tail. Continue shaping the butterfly's body.

This Fan-carver's third-hand (page 47) securely holds small items such as the butterfly. It allows both hands to be free while interlocking the wings.

Begin interlocking by moving the first blade to one side of the butterfly's head.

Move the second blade to the other side. The next (third) blade will interlock with the first blade.

Continue interlocking every other blade to its appropriate side until **2/3** of the blades are used. These are the two primary wings of the butterfly.

The remaining **1/3** of the blades will interlock in the same manner but separately from the primary wings. These will be the secondary set of wings.

For the antennae, cut two pieces of 20-gauge wire 1½″ long. Insert them into the butterfly's head. It is best to do this while the wood is still moist.

Once completed, position the two-sets of wings to be in line with the body.

A butterfly with four wings.

Butterfly Varieties

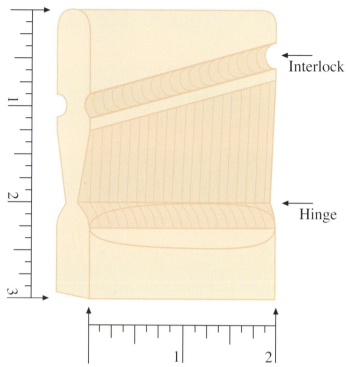

The interlock measurement of this butterfly is *reversed* to the one on page 130. (It is ½" on the head side and 1" on the tail side). Thus, it subtly creates a different butterfly …a new species.

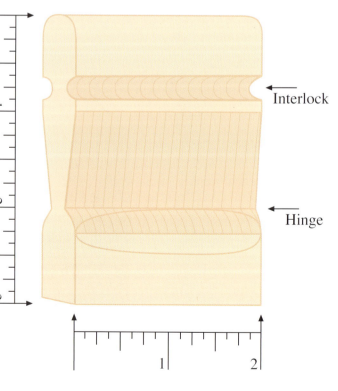

The interlock measurement of this butterfly is straight across the blank. (It is ¾" on the head side and ¾" on the tail side). Another *species* created!

...More Creations

...More Rived Items
Chapter Seven

Saint Tuomas Cross by Heikki Niskanen of Siilinjärvi, Finland

Sweden — Lamp shades in central Finland

Sweden — Roosters by Jiri Stoklasa of Banska Bystrica, Slovakia

136

Finland

Germany

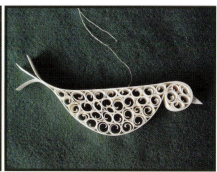
Germany

Germany

Germany

Germany

Tree (left) and sheep by Victor Hukka of Kerkonjoensuu, Finland

Oops ...but it's OK

Chapter Eight

Mistakes can happen! When they do, don't be eager to throw the carving away. Fan-carving is very forgiving.

Oops #1

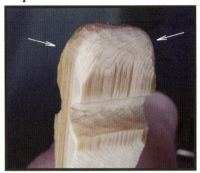

The ends are rounded off. This can happen while rounding off the rough-cut top end. It is best to leave the sides straight and flat. This is where the fibers are rived/split. It can be rived with sides rounded, but it is not fun to do. Besides that, the shape of those end blades will not be uniform with the others and may distort the pattern. They will probably be cut off.

Oops #2

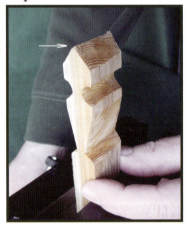

A pointed end can create some unique designs. *But*, it has a small viewing area when determining the thickness of the blade while riving. When the knife is tipped back to gauge the blade thickness, there is only one small point to view. It is something to be aware of when using this pointed design.

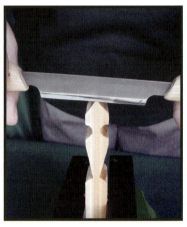

Oops #3

The interlock is not aligned. The right side is higher than the left side.

The fan looks O.K., but when the blades are interlocked they are slightly off-center. This creates a flowing pattern within the design. It offers an illusion of movement from one end to the other.

Oops #4

The interlock cut is off-center. The left side is cut too far into the center. The right side is shallow.

Once fanned, the off-center is noticable only on the end blade of the right side. The off-center of the other blades is hidden behind the next blade due to the interlocking process.

Another feature is apparent as well. Notice the nice edge line at the bottom of the interlock. The top of the interlock does *not* exhibit the same crisp edge. If the interlock was centered, the top and bottom would be uniform.

Oops #5

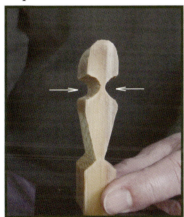

The interlock is too narrow before the blades are rived.

Even though the first few blades will probably rive O.K., the top will eventually begin to wobble. It is difficult to rive when this happens.

Oops #6

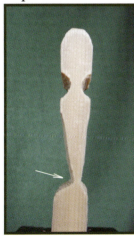

The hinge is off-center. The left side is cut too far into the center. The right side is shallow.

The fanning process is still O.K. The off-centered hinge causes the fan to be off-center at the base/handle. To compensate for this, the handle can be styled into a unique design.

Oops #7

The hinge is not aligned. The left side is lower than the right side. This creates an *undercut*.

When riving the fibers, the blades usually fall off. However, if they are held by a fiber, as in this case, the final product will be fragile. Once dried, a slight bump can cause the blades to fall off.

Oops #8

The hinge is rounded. There is no crisp V-cut to serve as a *stop-cut* when splitting the blades. Without the stop-cut, the knife tends to stop short of the hinge. This is more evident as more blades are rived. Once fanned, there is no nice hinge line that adds to the composition of the pattern. It is just there …rather blah!

Oops #9

The slight taper is omitted at the hinge. Instead of a wide V with a short side, the bottom side is *straight* to the edge. With no taper to relieve the pressure when riving, the blades tend to bind up, especially near the back. Sometimes the entire blank can split into two pieces! Remember, the wood is wet and long-fibered.

Oops #10

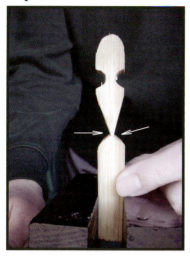

The hinge is very narrow before riving.

The first blades may rive O.K. But eventually, the very thin hinge will begin to wobble. It is not much fun trying to control the blank while splitting the fibers down to the hinge.

Oops #11

Rived blades are very thick. There are only seven blades here where there could be a minimum of twenty-one. The knife was *not* tipped back to gauge the blade thickness.

Thick blades can be interlocked. However, they do not fit nicely together to form a delicate pattern.

Oops #12

The blades are thin at the top and thick at the bottom. This is due to a gap between the flat back of the drawknife and the wood. The rive was started straight at the top. However, at the interlock, the knife was tipped forward. That created a gap and caused the knife to go off-fiber.

By flexing these irregular blades forward, the *cut through* fibers are revealed.

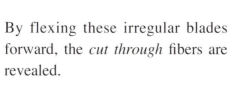

Bibliography

Andree-Eysn, Marie. *Volkskundliches aus dem bayrisch-österreichischen Alpengebiet*. Braunschwieg, Germany: Friedrich Vieweg & Sohn GmbH, 1910.

Bogataj, Prof. Dr. Janez. *Handicrafts of Slovenia*. Ljubljana, Slovenia: Rokus Pub. Hs. Ltd., 1999.

Cagner, Ewert and Axel-Nilsson, Dr. Göran and Sandblad, Dr. Henrik. *Swedish Christmas*. Gothenburg, Sweden: Tre Tryckare, 1954.

Eskeröd, Albert. *Fågelmakaren och Hans Fåglar*. Stockholm, Sweden: Nordiska Museet, 1957.

Eskeröd, Albert. *Swedish Folk Art*. Stockholm, Sweden: Nordiska, Museet, 1964.

Hammarstedt, N.E. *Fågeln med segerstenen sprängörten och lifsämnet*. Stockholm, Sweden: Nordiska Museet, 1903. (The Bird with the Victory Stone).

Hammarstedt, N.E. *Fataburen*. "Inspirationsfågeln." Kulturhistorisk, Tidskrift, Issue 1, Stockholm, Sweden: Nordiska Museet, 1908. (The Bird of Inspiration).

Johansson, Greta. *Slojd med ryska traditioner Tre generationer spanfagelmakare. Hemslojdem*. Sweden: 1993/6.

Johnson, Hugh. *The International Book of Trees*. New York: Bonanza Books, 1980.

Mielke, Dr. Heinz-Peter. *Kriegsgefangenen Arbeiten aus zwei Jahrhunferten*. West Germany: Grafik-Druck KG Müsers, 1987.

Milovsky, Alexander. *Keepers of Beauty*. "Seven blows of the Axe." by Alexander Petukhov. Leningrad, Russia: Aurora Art Publishers, 1983.

Nokelainen, Joel. *Vuolukirja*. Finland: 1996.

Nylén, Anna-Maja. *Swedish Handcraft*. New York: Van Nostrand Reinhold Co., 1977.

Outdoor World, Editors of. *Trees of America*. Waukesha, Wisconsin: Country Beautiful Corp.,1973.

Plath, Iona. *The Decorative Arts of Sweden*. New York: Charles Scribner's Sons, 1948.

Redaktör, Katarina Ågren. *Julträd och julkrus*. Växjö, Sweden: Grafiska Punkten, 2001.

Russell, Howard. *Carving The Wood of the World Vol. 1*. Ontario, Canada: 2004.
Russell, Howard. *Carving The Wood of the World Vol. 2*. Ontario, Canada: 2006.

Steffa, Liisa ja Tim. *Muisto Syväriltä sota-ajan puhdetyöt*. Keuruu, Finland: 1981.

Hansmann, Liselotte & Kriss-Rettenbeck, Lenz. *Amulet • Magie • Talisman*. Zwickau, Germany: Westermann Druck, 1977.

Vilkuna, Prof. Janne. *Christmas in Southwest Häme*. "Bird with Whittled Wings." Lounais-Hämeen Joule 1980.

INTERVIEWS:
Mojca Racic, Librarian, Slovenian Ethnographic Museum, Ljubljana, Slovenia
Barbara Sosic, Archival curator, Slovenian Ethnographic Museum, Ljubljana, Slovenia
Dr. Herlinde Menardi, Museum Curator, Tiroler Volkskunstmuseum, Innsbruck, Austria
Dr. Eberle Martin, Museum Curator, Städtisches Museum, Braunschweig, Germany
Mr. Jan Kube, Military historian, Sugenheim, Germany
Margrit Kempgen, church council advisor, Görlitz, Germany
Janne Vilkuna, professor of museology at Jyväskylä University, Finland
Sanna Koponen, museum director, Peuran museo, Rautalampi, Finland

*Through you,
this Old World folk art
lives on...*

...Sally and David